Theme Park Babylon

The Novel

Dale M. Brumfield

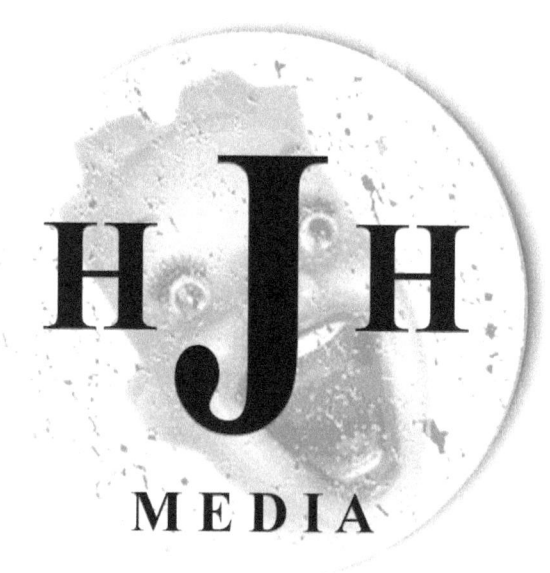

Richmond, Virginia, USA

Copyright © 2019 by Dale M. Brumfield

All rights reserved. No part of this publication may be reproduced, distributed or transmitted in any form or by any means, without prior written permission.

HJH Media
Richmond, Va.
HJHMedia@mail.com
www.dalebrumfield.net

Publisher's Note: This is a work of fiction. Names, characters, places, and incidents are a product of the author's imagination. Locales and public names are sometimes used for atmospheric purposes. Any resemblance to actual people, living or dead, or to businesses, companies, events, institutions, or locales is completely coincidental.

Manufactured in the United States of America.
First paperback edition, 2019

Cover art by Hunter Brumfield @Tidal Wave Studio
Burkewood Fun Park colophon image by Doug Dobey

Portions of this novel were released as an electronic version only in 2011 under the name "Bad Day at the Amusement Park."

10 9 8 7 6 5 4 3 2 1
Library of Congress Cataloguing information
Brumfield, Dale.
Theme Park Babylon: the novel / by Dale M. Brumfield
p.cm. Amusement parks / travel / fiction
ISBN-13: 978-0-578-57029-7 (paperback)
Former ASIN: B005AXY63Y (electronic)

*Welcome to Burkewood Fun Park –
Where there's fun around every corner!* ™

Also by Dale M. Brumfield
#10years10books

Memoir

Three Buck Naked Commodes: and 18 More Tales from a Small Town

Fiction

Remnants: A Novel about God, Insurance and Quality Floorcoverings

Trapped Under the Pack-Ice (eBook)

Bad Day at the Amusement Park (eBook)

Standers

Naked Savages

Non-fiction

Richmond Independent Press: A History of the Underground Zine Scene

Independent Press in D.C. and Virginia: An Underground History

Virginia State Penitentiary: A Notorious History

Anthologies

Richmond Macabre

Richmond Macabre II

Web

http://www.dalebrumfield.net

Staunton News-Leader https://www.newsleader.com/

https://medium.com/@dalebrumfield

Theme Park Babylon: the blog

https://www.instagram.com/brumfield.dale

https://www.facebook.com/dale.brumfield.1

Keep your arms and legs inside the vehicle

NOVEL RE-WRITES are like theme park rides, in that they may cycle between teen thrill and family attraction. This one is no different.

When written in 2010, then released in 2011 exclusively as an eBook for Kindle and Nook, "Bad Day at the Amusement Park" was a bold personal experiment, intended to capitalize on the predicted decline of print media and the exploding phenomenon of digital readers.

The story, based on my twenty years in the industry, was rough, loud and vulgar. It roared off the eReader screen in a stream of consciousness style intended to capture the bizarre environment of the subject matter while reveling in the brave new world of digital publishing. It was teen thrill.

Now, eight years, nine books and an MFA degree in fiction later, cooler heads have prevailed. I believe the story is better suited to the family attraction world of print.

Book publishing has made great strides since 2011, when this short novel first appeared under its previous name. Today, traditional big-box publishers that would never touch this work for a variety of lame and nonsensical excuses ("Sorry, we have no idea how to market this") have lost ground to smaller imprints that can publish for a fraction of the cost, yet still make professionally-produced books available worldwide through the traditional wholesalers. High-quality printing facilities print them at a moment's notice as the order comes in, and readers have a factory-fresh copy almost overnight.

Snooty traditionalists who think book publishing should be done today the way it was done in 1972 scoff at print-on-demand as not "real publishing," but 2019's casual reader (myself included) cannot distinguish if this book being read right now was printed by Simon & Schuster, Random House, Harper or HJH Media. There are publishing options available to authors today that they never had in 2011. Royalties are 25 percent higher. A savvy and determined writer should take crazy advantage of these options.

So here we are. 2011's "Bad Day at the Amusement Park" has been extensively re-written, revised, updated, edited and released as "Theme Park Babylon." More background is provided. New characters are introduced, others fleshed out and at least one eliminated entirely. The plot is enhanced. Holes and loose threads are (hopefully) closed and fixed. Confusing and overlapping dialogue is clarified. It is a new, personality-based lease on life as a more traditional, family-friendly attraction rather than the eccentric digital teen thrill product of 2011.

Also, don't tell anyone, but I am working to make this into a television series. Don't laugh. Or rather, do laugh – with the book. Not at me.

It is my sincere pleasure to bring to you this story, based on my experiences in the theme park business. I hope you like it and tell your friends. And be sure to peruse the most popular theme park blog in America, "Theme Park Babylon: the blog" at www.dalebrumfield.net.

Now, please turn the page on your right and enjoy the rest of your day.

Dale M. Brumfield
#10years10books.
#Americangrotesk
September 15, 2019

Chapter 1: in which I am interviewed

"YOU KNOW THE DIFFERENCE between a hammer and a screwdriver?"

"Yes, I do."

"Come on in this Saturday morning. I'll meet you at the guard shack at 5:20 a.m."

Chapter 2: in which I am stranded at a guard shack in the rain waiting for my ride

MY NEW JOB AT BURKEWOOD FUN PARK started promptly at 5:20 a.m. on March 27, 1980 at a bench outside a guard gate as I waited for my boss to come get me.

Today was opening day of the season and it was bitter cold, windy and raining. I felt like the last frozen yogurt raisin waiting to be picked up by the seagulls who gathered in a tight group a few hundred feet away near my lonely car, looking around at nothing at all, like they were waiting to be picked up as well.

We were all suffering similar indignities.

One of the guards looked at me. "Who's coming for you?"

He was past retirement age and his name tag read Lloyd. He had a big square face, covered in what they used to call gin blossoms back when alcoholism was funny. The other guard was inside the guard shack on the phone. His voice was deep, loud and staccato. People were already calling to see if the park was going to be open on such a horrible day. He barked and yipped inside the shack.

"Walter Baxter," I answered.

Gin blossom Lloyd the guard looked deep in thought. "Walter Baxter? What department is that? Food service?"

"No. Ride maintenance."

"Baxter ... *Baxter* ... okay, wait there on that bench."

It was dark as hell with the heavy cloud cover and rain. It was as if time had not started yet, that I was standing in the Earth without form, and void, just before God said let there be light.

While I hated the hours and the weather, I was still enthusiastic about this particular job. As a kid I visited this park often in the summer with family and friends. I became a ride geek, riding, reading and absorbing intricate details of the rides and offering them up whether people wanted to hear them or not.

Once I interviewed a former employee for our high school newspaper, and I learned how a guy came from Switzerland in the winter who could seamlessly cut then splice the Skyride cable. I knew the names of every board and part of a wooden roller coaster – ribbons, bents, stompers, batter braces, chicken feet, ledgers, chords, and so on.

I knew that each Scrambler pod traced a 24-point "star" during each cycle, and that the pods went from zero to twenty-five miles-per-hour in two seconds, making it one of the fastest accelerating rides in the park. I knew that Philadelphia Toboggan Company Carousels were renowned for their exquisite carving, lavish crestings and magnificent animals. I knew that master carver John Zalar established that characteristic design and style of carousel horses for many years.

I memorized this minutia so no one else had to. So, the opportunity to work there and learn even more inside stories of these rides was quite appealing to me.

As gin blossom Lloyd looked around, as if trying to find someone in a crowd of no one, the other guard bulldozed his way out of the shed. He was stumpy and brash, like an angry farm dog. There was no one there but a hundred acres of lined, lumpy asphalt, poured over what prior to the 1940s was 350 years of southern Virginia tobacco rows, stretching for what seemed to be miles into the void. The guard gate was barely illuminated by a humming sodium vapor lamp at the top of a tall aluminum pole.

The phone rang.

"Damn that phone!" The short farm dog guard barked as he barged back into the shed.

"That fella, he's crazier than I am," Lloyd observed, as he dutifully scanned the empty parking lot that he couldn't even see in the torrential rain. "But he's a good guard. A few years back a retired employee drove in here naked. I didn't see him, but Walt did. He said that fella was naked."

And darkness moved on the face of the waters.

"Yes. No. Far as I know the park will be open." The farm dog guard slammed the phone and barged back out the door as if he was on a short leash under the little canopy that barely kept the three of us out of the driving rain, which seemed to be getting worse. "That phone's a hotline this morning."

It was 5:28. I was supposed to start work at 5:30. I was getting nervous.

Gin blossom Lloyd looked at me. "Who did you say was supposed to get you?"

"Walter Baxter,"

"And what department?"

For God's sake. "Ride maintenance."

Lloyd moved his lips as he silently repeated the name. "Okay, wait there on the bench."

I got nowhere else to be.

A gust of wind blew cold rain in on me. The guards inched closer to the door. I watched water boil down a half-clogged storm drain. A tiny space heater glowed under a desk inside the shack.

The phone rang again.

"Hotline!" the farm dog guard sputtered as he bulldozed back inside. "Hotline!"

Lloyd joined in the fun. "Hotline," he too repeated. "Hotline …"

Lloyd pushed his hands into his pockets and stared into the abyss as the farm dog guard repeated almost verbatim the previous call. "Yes. Yes. Far as I know the park will be open." He hung up and stormed out as thunder rolled somewhere in the black horizon. This time I saw his nametag read Walt. "I don't mind the heat but I do not like this cold," he growled.

It was now 5:30 a.m. Technically I was on the clock, earning four dollars an hour. I peeked over toward the huge maintenance building looking for a sign of life. Nothing. Walter did say I started at 5:30, right? He did say today, right? Suddenly I was unsure of my own name or my purpose in life.

God had yet to make living things, other than me, Lloyd and Walt.

Lloyd squinted at the parking lot, then at me. "Did your fella say he would meet you at the guard shack?"

"Yes, sir."

A flash of headlights appeared from behind the gate.

God said let there be light.

"Maybe this is your fella."

A thirty-year-old pickup truck crept through the rain past the guard shack, its wipers thumping furiously. The truck was in hideous shape, covered bumper to bumper in dents and scratches. It sat absurdly low in the back. A grease pump and storage tank filled the rear bed.

Three guys were stuffed in the cab, bundled in corduroy coats, caps and rain gear. They looked miserable, like a train car load of refugees passing through Poland in 1943. The one in the middle had a small cup of coffee in his hand. They stared through the filthy window at me as they crept by, their unfocused headlights cutting in opposing directions through the foggy cold rain, like movie premiere searchlights stuck out of position.

That was not my fella.

"That grease truck stinks," Lloyd remarked as he waved them through. "I couldn't pump grease all day."

"How about Helen at the truck stop buffet?" Walt sputtered with a laugh. "You pump her all day?"

Lloyd didn't return the laugh. "Ah hell Walt, I can't pump anything all day no more. Much less Helen. All that thing is good for is running water through it."

The phone rang. Thank God.

"Hotline! Hotline! ... Hotline!" they both chimed in. It was their joke, and they were not going to let go.

The stinking grease truck disappeared somewhere in the black parking lot, swallowed up by formless sheets of cold rain. Once again Lloyd, Walt and I, at guard shack 3, were the only living things in this whole park. In the entire world.

Lloyd turned to me. "I think your fella forgot about you."

I must have made quite an impression at the interview.

"Far as I know the park will be open."

"What department did you say he was in? Food service?"

"Ride maintenance."

"And when did he tell you he would pick you up?"

"Around 5:20."

"Well, it's 5:35 now." Lloyd looked at his watch then at me, like being stranded was my fault.

The phone rang.

"Goddamn! Hotline! Hotline! Hotline!"

"Hotline!"

"Who?" Walt the angry farm dog guard walked to the door and looked at me, the phone's curly cord stretched all the way out like he was pulling taut on his collar chain while tied to the only tree left in the trailer park. "What's your name, son?"

"Dale."

Walt squinted. "He said his name is Dave … uh-huh … yea. No."

"Dale, not Dave," I said louder.

"Huh?"

"Dale, not Dave. My name is Dale."

Walt corrected himself. "He said his name is not Dave. Okay. Okay."

Lloyd squinted into the lot. Maybe he saw something in the dark that time. Maybe a terrorist carrying a bomb was trying to sneak into an empty amusement park on foot at 5:36 a.m. in driving rain on the coldest March day in twenty-one years, and Lloyd was going to catch him. And he was going to show his boss and justify his presence there.

Walt hung up the phone. "That was the attendant over in the ride maintenance shop. He said this Walter fella will be here in a minute to pick you up. He said he forgot you were out here."

Christ.

The phone rang yet again.

"Damn! Hotline! Hotline! Hotline!"

Lloyd looked at me with hope. "Well, at least we know your fella is coming to pick you up. You won't have to wait here with us all day. Although we get off work in eighteen – no, sixteen minutes."

Walt the farm dog guard came back to the door and stood for a minute. "You know, somebody calls you on the phone ... they want something."

I was almost impressed by his powers of deduction. "That's almost always the case."

It was raining buckets. Realistically, I never wanted to go home worse in my life but I had to have this job. This was 1980, there was a recession and jobs were scarce. I graduated from a major university four months earlier with a Bachelor of Science degree. I sent out fifty letters and sat in over a dozen interviews but received not one job offer. My 45-second interview with Walter was lucky interview number 13.

This job was only four days a week, and only paid four bucks an hour, but I had no choice. I was broke. I was driving an uninsured car, and eating macaroni in an apartment where I was at risk of eviction.

My senior year in school I regretfully concentrated on parties, politics, girls, pot and beer – everything except cultivating a post-graduation career. I figured the degree would open doors regardless of my behavior. It didn't happen. This day I had no party, no girls, no pot, no beer and worse, no income.

The job market was awful. Damn Reagan in the White House.

Lloyd adjusted his cap. His most impressive gin blossom was on his bulbous nose. It was like a little pal. He looked out across the vast expanse of parking lot. "This is a terrible day to open," he mused. "Ain't nobody coming today. Why they even bothering?"

"No, no," Walt barked back, "people are crazy. They'll come if it was a cyclone. I seen them stand in line to ride in weather worse than this."

Gin blossom Lloyd adjusted his cap once more and looked at me. "You going to be temporary? Full time? Part time? Contractor? Seasonal?"

All good questions. "I really don't know," I responded.

"This is a good place to work full-time if you can get it," Lloyd explained. "The pay ain't great but they buy and wash our uniforms. And last Christmas they backed a chicken truck into the carpenter shop, and we sat on lumber stacks and ate free chicken."

"It was good chicken," Walt added, "and even better when it's free."

"Yea, it was awful good chicken. And good rolls too. What department will you be in? Food service?"

"Ride maintenance."

"Who will you be working for?"

"Walter Baxter."

Lloyd paused. "He was going to pick you up, but he forgot."

Nothing gets by you, Lloyd. Except maybe a naked retired employee.

Lloyd looked at Walt. "Hey Walt, remember what today is?"

Walt thought for a moment. "Well, it's the thirtieth season of the park ... but isn't it your thirtieth work anniversary too?"

Lloyd nodded proudly. "Indeed it is! I started working here March 27, 1950. Doing the exact same thing I'm doing right now, overnight gate security, right here at this gate."

My sense of hope plummeted with Lloyd's career work history as suddenly another set of lights appeared from behind the maintenance building. They pulled ahead a bit then stopped. Then pulled ahead, stopped and cut off. Lloyd, Walt and I watched the halting headlights silently. It looked like somebody learning to drive a stick. Then through the pounding deluge, we heard the vehicle restart and pull over to the guard shack. It hit the semi-stopped up storm drain cover and splashed the side of the shack before stopping beside my bench.

"Congratulations, Lloyd!" Walt exclaimed. "I guess you'll be doing some celebrating when you get off."

"I'll be meeting up with Helen at the truck stop breakfast buffet first," Lloyd winked. "Then we'll share a bottle of liquid celebration in my car."

It was a white truck with Burkewood Fun Park written on the door, with that creepy image of the laughing kid. The passenger window rolled down and a man with yellow teeth and a whole lot of red gums leaned over.

"You Dave?"

"I'm Dale."

"This might be your fella," Lloyd commented from behind my back before he turned back to his partner, Walt. "101 proof celebration!"

"Walter told me to pick you up and take you with me," the gummy man shouted to me through the rain. "Hop in."

Lloyd looked at me earnestly. "Is this the fella you're supposed to go with?"

"Close enough," I answered as the gummy man opened the passenger door from the inside. At this point, I would have squeezed in that grease truck.

The phone rang one last time.

"Hotline! Hotline! Hotline! Hotline!"

I ducked out into the pouring rain and jumped inside the pickup. It smelled a bit like stale amusement park fried something. The defroster was blasting out 100,000 BTUs of freezing air. I had to pull my coat a little tighter.

"I'm Lump," the gummy man informed me as we shook hands. "That's what everybody calls me. Our boss, Walter, is tied up at the Scrambler. Something happened down there yesterday when they were filming a commercial. He told me to carry you down there. I got to stop by the shop and get my toolbox. You want a coffee?"

"I'd love one," I sighed, relieved to be away from Lloyd and Walt. "Why do they call you Lump?"

"Um, long story," Lump answered with a grimace. "Something come up once in ... well, I made the mistake of asking one of the guys to look at something and see if it was bleeding. I've never lived it down."

I had to ask.

Lump did a U-turn at the edge of the thousand-acre parking lot but had to stop, back up and try again. A thousand acres of asphalt to make a U-turn and he had to back up and try again. We crept back through the guard gate, waving at Lloyd, who nodded as he diligently guarded his post from the huddled seagulls a thousand feet away and that imaginary terrorist trying to sneak in under the humming sodium vapor pole light.

You know, somebody calls you on the phone, they want something.

Chapter 3: in which I meet a gentleman named Barnyard who shows me how not to inspect a wooden roller coaster

LUMP DROVE THE TRUCK slowly around the maintenance building, the wipers beating back and forth too fast in the rain and the defroster blasting an icy blast of sweet, stinking antifreeze. He pulled through a big door into a huge shop, filled with workbenches, hoists and tackles. The rain suddenly stopped, but the wipers kept beating until he shut off the engine.

The shop was cluttered with several types of industrial machines, all designed to assist in the rides maintenance process. I saw a band saw, a drill press, a Rockwood metal lathe and a hydraulic press.

At one end of the wall was an opening into a huge tool and parts storage area, covered with a sliding chain link Dutch door. This was the tool cage, and it held dozens of oversize hand tools, power tools and ride parts. To the left was a normal chain link door with a huge padlock to keep out riff-raff. The top half was open and an older, distressed guy in a cowboy hat stood inside looking at us.

His body said tool cage attendant but his face said imprisonment.

Lump cut off the truck and he and I got out, He walked over to a bench containing cabinets underneath. He opened one and hoisted out a huge toolbox painted completely in grey primer. "Run over yonder to the tool cage and tell Tex to give you a drill motor and an extension cord."

I did as I was instructed. "Hello there, young man," the cowboy hat announced to me. "You can call me Tex, everybody else does. Shitty weather this morning Jesus I hate coming to this job in this weather. I live eighty-six miles away and I have to get up at 3:00 a.m. to get here by 5:00." His name tag verified his name as Tex.

"I'm Dale." We shook hands through the cage window. "Apparently I need a drill motor and a cord."

"Three-eighths or half-inch?"

What was this man inside this cage asking me?

"I ... don't know."

"Lump, do I give this young man a three-eighths motor or a half-inch motor?" Tex shouted just past my clueless head. "He has no idea what I'm talking about. And how long a cord you need?"

"Half-inch I reckon," Lump drawled as he dropped his grey spray-painted toolbox in the dripping truck bed. "A fifty-foot cord will do it."

"We ain't got no more drill motors but I got a cord."

"Well shit, Tex," Lump answered, "a cord don't do us no good without a drill motor."

Tex wasn't convinced. "What size drill bit you want for the motor?"

Lump walked to the window. "A bit won't do us no good neither without a motor. What the hell's wrong with you?"

Suddenly a phone inside the cage rang.

Hotline, I whispered to myself as Tex answered.

"Tool cage. Yea he's here. Phone, Lump." Tex handed the receiver through the window to Lump.

I listened in fascination as Lump engaged in a conversation using terms that seemed strangely foreign. "Hello? Yea I got him. But there's no more motors in the tool cage. I'll look in our gang box. Okay ... at the Gator? I'll drop him on my way back. Why did they run the rides last night? We had them all signed off now we got to check them again? Shit! Filming commercials? I'll be ... alright."

Lump handed the phone back to Tex and looked at me. "You got your coffee yet?"

"No."

"Come on."

I followed Lump across the shop through a door on a far wall into a break room. The downside of being the brand-new guy at a job was that I had to follow somebody else like a puppy because I could not anticipate where they would go next. If I got in front I would be perceived as arrogant, and the guy could veer off and go somewhere else leaving me walking by myself into parts unknown.

Instead we walked inside the break room. There were four picnic tables, each with an overflowing ashtray. A sad sandwich sat on one of the tables on a napkin. It looked several days old. The top slice of bread curled up like a wet roofing shingle. An old fridge wheezed against an opposite wall beside a countertop and sink. A hand-written sign taped to the door warned everyone to not eat someone else's lunch.

"You need to see Judy when she comes in at 7:00," Lump instructed. "She pretty much runs the department. She'll get you a time card and do your maintenance orientation."

"What does maintenance orientation consist of?" I pictured an all-day seminar, with charts and graphs and handbooks and warnings and educational filmstrips and guest speakers but I guessed that imagery was most likely incorrect.

Lump handed me an empty coffee pot and motioned for me to fill it in the sink. "She'll say don't pick up money under a ride. Clock in on time. Don't do anything stupid. That's about it."

Bingo.

He put a filter in the basket then poured in a package of Maxwell House instant coffee. He closed the basket and I handed him the pot. He poured the water in and watched. He was making a pot of instant coffee in a real coffee coffeemaker.

"She's good looking as shit," he added as an afterthought.

It was a good thing he was there to guide me, otherwise I would have screwed this up. Maybe coffee will get covered in orientation.

"Why am I going to the Gator?" I asked. The water started streaming through the instant coffee and filling the pot. I thought I could smell that sandwich but not the coffee.

"Walter said you were going down there with Barnyard to help him check it," Lump explained. "Damn TV people here last night takin' pictures and film and shit running all the rides so now we got to check everything again. We had the rides all ready to go then they ran them."

"Is every ride checked again after every time it runs?"

"Yep." Suddenly Lump's shirt looked like he had worn it for a week.

"What's a Barnyard?" I queried.

"His name's Bradley. He checks the wood coaster. We call him Barnyard. Don't even know why. His toolbox is a plastic five-gallon bucket. He's a crazy sumbitch but a decent mechanic."

The Gator was a figure-8 style wood coaster built in the early 1960s at a time when most parks nationwide were tearing down wood coasters. It was patterned after a coaster built in 1932 in Lubbock, Texas. The Gator was about 3,500 feet long, and its highest hill was eighty-six feet tall. It hit sixty miles-per-hour on a hot day. Many guests complained it was too rough. I was a real coaster trivia expert.

After a few minutes, the instant coffee was ready. I heard a couple more guys out in the shop asking for drill motors and being told by Tex there were no more but he had plenty of cords. Screw that, they insisted, what good is a cord without a drill motor?

In 1972, a Gator operator accidentally ran two trainloads of people together. No one was killed but over twenty-five people were injured, some seriously. The accident prompted major changes in coaster braking systems. It was an effective and common-sense change – in the old days the brakes stayed open and the operator pushed a button to close them. After the change, the brakes stayed closed and the operator had to push a button to open them. Smart.

I poured a cup of brewed instant coffee and it tasted like that foam that bubbles out of an old tractor battery in a landfill. I shook, tore and dumped in three cream packets. The powdered cream came out in clumps. It was four months out of date, but at least my coffee tasted better.

Lump motioned to a nearby door. "Toilet's over yonder if ya gotta go."

"I'm fine."

"Somebody went in that toilet last Friday and took the dump of a lifetime," Lump informed me, giving me information that I would unfortunately carry with me throughout my professional career. "It wouldn't flush. It looked like they gave birth to a baby seal. Maybe it was the Craft-Tech tool guy. He would do something like that."

Oh God please stop.

"Walter had to go in there and beat it up with a coat hanger just so it would …" Lump scrunched his face in a knot and heaved in his mouth just a little, like he just made himself sick talking about it. Then he heaved again.

My coffee suddenly tasted a little bit worse. In fact, my whole life was suddenly a little bit worse.

I heard voices. "I need a drill, not a cord, you dumbass." Somebody was getting up in Tex's face when we walked with our nasty coffee back into the shop, me shuddering from Lump's story.

"Over yonder's the time clock," Lump explained as he pointed on the wall to an obvious time clock surrounded on both sides by racks containing time cards. "Punch in when you get here but not more than five minutes before your shift. Don't punch in late because it punches red. Dink comes out and looks for all the red ones then finds those guys and yells at them for punching late. Judy will go over that with you."

"What's a Dink?" I asked. This job was filled with foreign terms. The time clock thunked over to 5:50 a.m.

"The maintenance manager," Lump explained. "Walter's boss. He's foreign or maybe from another country. His real name's Dinklin I think. He's been here since day one and he hates everybody. It's best to stay away from him."

To the right of the time clock was a bulletin board with several company flyers and reminders tacked on. A huge workman's compensation notice dominated the center. You have rights, it proclaimed. A few bulk printed safety flyers that looked like they had been there for decades were pinned in the corners. "Wear your hard hat and keep the head you have under it" warned one left over from construction days. Another said, "Give yourself a hand and wear your gloves." Somebody had a 1979 Dodge Dart for sale that "don't run." A 1977 Pontiac J-2000 advertised in a child's handwriting needed tires, a water pump, alternator, heater core and the head liner "stapled back up." Otherwise it "ran like a brand new one."

Lump got in the truck first and following new guy protocol I dutifully got in second. "Ah damn this weather," he moaned as he started the truck and backed out into the black driving storm, flipping the wipers to warp speed and cranking the defroster to gale. The windshield immediately fogged over opaque from the blast of frigid air. Lump wiped a small opening in the center of the windshield with his hand. He moaned again as he sipped his nasty instant coffee.

"I'll drop you at the Gator with Barnyard."

"I can't wait to meet this Barnyard gentleman and possibly discuss politics or philosophy with him."

"Huh? Yea." Lump made a right turn and dumped his coffee in his lap. "Ow dammit!" he bellowed. "Dammit!" Instead of pulling over he grabbed a couple of shop rags and stuffed his crotch with them as he weaved around the area outside the shop. I wanted to laugh but thought otherwise. Lump was in scalding pain.

Finally, he stopped the truck. "I forgot to get the drill out of the gang box. I'll drop you off with Barnyard and come back. I got to change pants anyhow."

Cursing and complaining of his "burned grinds," Lump drove past a huge, magnificent, state-of-the-art trash compactor then turned left onto a paved service road, the truck now smelling of spilled instant coffee, which was actually a bit of an improvement. We drove in the cold rain past some woods, crossed over a former narrow-gauge railroad then turned left on a rough gravel drive. I noticed looming wooden pillars on either side. We were driving underneath a roller coaster. It was ominous and spooky.

Lump pulled up beside a wooden building, labeled "motor house." Everything was pitch black in the rain, and I had no reference for where I was. "Barnyard's down here somewhere, probably up there in the station," he speculated. "Hop out and look around. You'll find him."

"Okay." I hopped out in the rain and trotted over to an overhang on the building and looked around per Lump's instruction as he backed back down the gravel road. The headlights illuminated a massive ghostly skeleton of pressure-treated timbers, nailed and bolted and stretching silently up into the foggy blackness just before he turned and disappeared.

I was in the dark, silent wet belly of a Gator.

There was no sign of Barnyard or anybody or anything else once the truck left. I was alone in the rain underneath a roller coaster. It was like being dropped at the edge of the Arctic Circle with orders to find the North Pole carrying nothing but a Yahtzee game.

Adjusting to the darkness and pulling my coat across my chest, I could make out a single illuminated exit sign in the dark through the structure so I walked toward it, crunching through gravel, figuring that must be the station.

I was in a cheesy horror movie, my car broken down on a back road at night. I was walking toward a lone farmhouse with a single light in the window.

I suddenly whacked my head on a horizontal board, just before I stumbled on a concrete footer that held one of the coaster's legs, then whacked my head again. Good grief, I was in an obstacle course – there were boards just above eye level, at ankle level and crisscrossing in front of me. The sign was looming closer. Was I headed into a trap?

Was this Barnyard waiting behind a post in the dark, with a rope and a meat hook?

Squatting like I was ducking bullets, I wound through the pressure-treated maze to a set of stairs at the foot of another large wooden building. I recognized it as the Gator station, barely illuminated inside by maintenance lights. I jogged up the stairs into the building, more just to get out of the cold rain than go to work.

Once in the station, things were familiar – I had been here many times as a rider. A coaster train painted light blue sat in front of the loading gates. Three lap restraints were tied off with plastic trash bags. A white five-gallon former cole slaw bucket full of well-used tools sat beside a partially disassembled bagged lap bar.

How dystopian, I thought, to be inside a lonely roller coaster station with only the barest signs of previous human life. The rain beat mercilessly on the corrugated metal roof.

As I pondered the surrealness of my surroundings, I suddenly heard a muffled walkie-talkie radio bark from under the station somewhere. Somebody named 4-0 was calling somebody named 3-6, *scratch*.

A sign of life. There was another set of stairs by the operator's panel leading down underneath the station, so I walked slowly down them, thinking either a deformed post-apocalyptic mutant or my work partner was down there somewhere.

At the foot of the stairs, I found myself under the station, surrounded by a maze of sprinkler pipes, air lines, electrical pipe, conduit and other paraphernalia associated with roller coaster operation. The mechanism that opened and closed the loading gates was just over my head, about six feet up, a tangle of gears and hoses.

"4-0 to 3-6, *scratch*." I was closer.

The voice seemed to come from behind a door behind me labeled "Gator Electric."

"4-0 to 3-6, *scratch*."

I opened the door. The room was pitch-dark and a toasty eighty-five degrees. I felt for and flipped a light switch and lying in front of a floor-to-ceiling electrical panel was a short guy with his jacket rolled up under his head for a pillow. He looked deceased. Then he opened his eyes, snorted and scrambled to his feet.

"Jiminy Christmas who the hell are you I thought you were Dink," he sputtered.

"And I thought you were dead," I responded. "I'm new and I'm supposed to be helping you get this ride ready."

"Good God you scared the hell out of me."

"Sorry. Are you Barnyard?" I asked.

"I wasn't asleep." He snorted through his nose like he had bad sinus drainage but the *snock* sound was more like a nervous habit than an actual condition. "You're here, so come on up so we can finish inspection. I got seats to check."

"Are you radio 3-6?" I asked.

"Huh? My radio? Yea why?"

"Somebody named 4-0 was trying to call you."

"Oh, shit it was Dink. Screw him. I'll call him later."

I followed Barnyard up the steps back to the station. For a younger guy, he had an ass like a big old black bumblebee. His steel-toe safety shoes were completely rotten and wrapped with silver duct tape. We walked into the eerie station.

"Why don't you walk the tracks while I check the trains? *Snock*."

I was flummoxed as I looked out into the rainy darkness at the intimidating wood structure. "You are kidding right?" I asked. "I've never walked a coaster track in my life. It's raining and I can't see. I'd kill myself. What am I even walking it for?"

"We're supposed to walk the track every day before opening if it operated the day before," Barnyard explained. "We look for loose nails and bolts, and to make sure the steel track is tight at all the joints. Don't worry there's a catwalk all the way around. Forget it. I'm sure it's fine. I need to check this train."

Barnyard put the cover back on the lap bar mechanism he was working on after drowning it in WD-40. He walked over to his five-gallon bucket toolbox and retrieved a huge, ancient screwdriver. "When you check the trains, don't look down between the seat and back cushions."

I watched as he jammed his huge screwdriver down between the black vinyl pads and pried forward, looking intently down in the cracks. He went to the next one, then the next. On the third car, he blurted "ka-ching," reached down in the gap and retrieved a $5 bill.

"This ride can be a gold mine, but we're not supposed to pick up money," he explained. *Snock*. "It's so rough it shakes riders' money out of their pockets. You can get fired. Jeez I'm starving. I find watches, wallets and bills down in these cushions all the time. But you didn't hear that. I need to check the other train."

His tortured and contradictory explanation was like flipping a television channel – one spoken sentence had nothing to do with the last. I watched as Barnyard checked every seat but only found a few quarters after his $5 bill. He checked nothing else. He then walked over to the operator's panel, pulled his giant key ring off a belt loop and inserted a key labeled DH-28 into a key switch. He turned it and the operator's panel flashed and beeped to life.

"4-0 to 3-6, *scratch*."

"The boss is calling you," I noted.

"Damn radio," he muttered as he just turned it off.

"Screw walking the tracks in this weather," he stated. "They only ran three or four cycles for those commercials last night. The ride is built way stronger than it needs to be anyway. There's nothing wrong out there."

Noting a pressure indicator on the operator's panel, he picked up a house phone next to him and punched three numbers. "Holy moly there Andy!" he spoke into the phone in an exaggerated Amos n' Andy-style voice. "I gotta go down to the lodge hall!"

I could hear Tex shouting something similar from the other end. Apparently, this was a running riff between the two of them.

"Need some air at the Gator there, Andy," Barnyard continued in his best Kingfish voice. "I'm suffocatin' down here! Start the compressor there Andy!"

He hung up the phone and looked at me. "Tex up in the tool cage can turn on the compressors so we can start the rides," he explained. "We need 120 pounds of air pressure to run the ride. The whole park is on an air system loop. The brakes run on air. The ride won't start if there's no air. *Snock.*"

I pictured Tex back in the tool cage blowing into a pipe, sending air to the rides. In reality, he was flipping little toggle switches, remotely activating the big compressors that were scattered in series around the park.

"So, you don't think the track needs to be walked?" I asked. The air pipes under the station creaked as the pressure built. A dial on the operator's console slowly drifted up.

"Let me tell ya something about a roller coaster track," Barnyard pointed out, as if he suddenly was an authority. "It's built like a hundred times stronger than it needs to be. The ride is so strong I've been taking out one bolt a day where the track attaches to the intermediates just to prove that it's overbuilt. Right where it crosses over the tunnel.

It's crazy how strong it is. All month down here doing winter maintenance I took out a bolt every day and when we got the trains rebuilt and started cycling it was like they were never there. I could take out half this entire structure and it wouldn't make a shit bit of difference."

Suddenly the ride ready light came on. "Run up there at the end of the station and push that lift button," he instructed. I walked to the end of the station and depressed a button on a grey electrical box that was labeled dual dispatch. I heard the lift chain rattle to life. Barnyard pressed the dispatch button, and nothing happened.

"Dammit," he muttered. He hit the lap bar lock button five or six times. *Clunk clunk clunk clunk.* He then pressed dispatch. The big heavy baby blue train squeaked to a start and drifted out of the station, rolled around the first turn into the dark rain, rumbled across the transfer table then rolled out of sight. After a few seconds, I heard it clatter up onto the lift chain.

"Walter bring you down here?" Barnyard asked, staring at his grimy fingernails.

"No, somebody named Lump."

"That fuckin' Alabama hillbilly," Barnyard continued in his weird blather. "Lump ain't his real name, I think its Lawrence or something. I give him titty twisters. His titties stay black and blue all the time because of me. I reckon Walter's at the Scrambler. Some actor got hurt on it last night filming the commercial. It's cold as hell today. The pod popped open and threw him down on the concrete. I hear the sweep ran over him. *Snock.*

Ignoring Barnyard's snotty non-linear soliloquy, I stood at the end of the station listening to the train clatter and bang up the big lift hill. I knew from reading about wooden coasters that the banging sound is caused by steel pieces on the bottom of the train called anti-rollback dogs. They bang in and out of a step-like piece of angle iron running to the top of the hill. If the lift stops for whatever reason the anti-rollback dogs keep the train from rolling back down the hill.

"Ambulance took him to the hospital," Barnyard continued, still staring at his chewed-down fingernails. "Security guys were down on the ride at two in the morning scrubbing the blood off the cement pad."

At the top of the hill, when the chain dogs and the anti-rollback dogs released from the chain, the train was on its own, running strictly on gravity. Nobody could stop it even if they wanted to. I listened as the train disappeared off into the woods in the darkness, then as it returned at what seemed to be a thousand miles an hour, exiting a tunnel with a blast like a bullet train and roaring around a banked curve. The entire structure sagged and groaned with the fury of the thundering train.

"They don't know why the bucket latch popped open," Barnyard kept explaining. "If the guy would have stayed down on the pad he wouldn't have got hit. He tried to stand up and the ride hit him. Damn shame."

After the banked curve, the train made a horrible *blangalangalangalang* noise that didn't sound right even to me, the new guy, as it crossed over itself in the figure-8 configuration. Barnyard never looked up. Again, it disappeared into the rainy early morning dark, roaring loud then soft, loud then soft as it crested hills and negotiated dips and curves. A minute later it appeared at the end of a long straightaway at the end of the station and screeched to a stop. Where it sat.

Barnyard was no longer at the operator's panel. He had abandoned his post and walked down into the storage area near where Lump had dropped me off, prying his huge screwdriver down into the seat cushions of the red train, looking for loot that he was not supposed to be looking for. I stood there like an idiot, not knowing what to do. The train looked at me, wondering why it was sitting on the emergency brakes and not being moved down onto the trim brakes, then onto the station brakes.

I don't know anything, I admitted sheepishly. I'm the new guy.

Barnyard finally walked back up to the station when he finished digging through the seats. "Bunch of poor people rode that train yesterday," he complained. He approached the operator's panel and pushed a couple of buttons, releasing the brakes and sending the blue train drifting back down onto the next brake zone, then into the station, where it parked with a swish sound. Barnyard clicked off the panel and hung his key ring on his belt loop. *Snock*.

"I'll sign the sheet and we're done," he concluded. The "sheet" was a maintenance and inspection check sheet that listed all kinds of technical items that were, I presumed, supposed to be completed before the ride could open. Check bottom of trains. Check all wheels for tightness. Check all cotter keys and jam nuts. Ensure free travel of friction wheels and pickup wheels. Look for linear indications (cracks) and other abnormalities. Check.

"Why are these lap bars tied off with garbage bags?" I asked.

"Operators say they don't open," Barnyard sneered. "You just gotta pull them the right way. I hit the button five or six times they open right up. *Snock.*

The list went all the way to item 31. Barnyard did none of them but checked them all anyway without blinking, including walking the track. Check, check and check.

The only one he could have answered honestly was if all the seats were checked for lost money. Check.

Before we left Barnyard walked down the train and using a pocket knife cut all the trash bags off the defective lap bars.

"Good to go. Grab my toolbox," he commanded.

"Bucket," I corrected.

"Bucket, whatever," he replied with some impatience. I complied. I guess part of my responsibilities also included toting other guys' tool buckets.

"Good to go," he repeated as we exited the station back to his truck, parked at the guest entrance. *Snock.* The sky had gone from black to charcoal, and the rain let up a bit. It was still bitter cold as we wound slowly through the empty asphalt streets of the abandoned park in the cold truck.

"Break time," Barnyard announced as we arrived back at the shop.

Chapter 4: in which I experience the break room and learn park policy on picking up money

BARNYARD DROVE HIS TRUCK all the way into the shop like Lump did earlier. "Holy moly there Andy!" he shouted as he got out. Tex stuck his head around the corner of the tool cage at him. The shop was cool and drafty from having the big door open.

"Holy moly there, Kingfish!" He yelled back. "When are you going down to the lodge hall?"

Snock. Barnyard strolled into the break room. I followed him, as trailing new guy protocol dictated. That bare sandwich was still on the table. Two other guys were seated at one of the picnic tables, having coffee and a pack of nabs. One of them was obese with graying hair. The other was skinny and about 6'-4", with black hair and a push broom moustache. I caught the tail end of their conversation.

"... the cantaloupe had rolled under the spare tire," the tall one explained. "After two weeks in that hot trunk, it exploded. I had to call that company that cleans dead body smells for the coroner's office."

"So that's where the smell was coming from," the obese one confirmed.

"Fuck you Barnyard," the tall one suddenly growled when we came in. Maybe he was half-joking. Maybe not. It was impossible to tell.

"No, you'd probably just lay there," Barnyard replied. He walked straight into the bathroom without stopping. I stopped at the coffee pot, considering another cup. I didn't need to follow him into the bathroom. I wasn't that helpless.

"I'm Dave, but everybody calls me Mudflap," the tall guy stated to me as he stood and extended a hand. He did not explain the source of his unusual nickname. "This here is Bill – and we call him something else too."

"Stop," Bill warned.

I shook hands with them both. They were both soaking wet from inspecting rides in the downpour. I reluctantly got a cup of ghastly coffee and sat down at the table beside them.

"Slide that sandwich over out of your way," Bill suggested. It wasn't in my way but I did anyway. It was like nudging a tiny corpse.

"Why did Walter stick you with Barnyard?" Mudflap asked. "He trying to run you off your first day on the job?"

"I guess he thought he needed help getting the Gator running in this rain," I speculated, although judging by Barnyard's inspection skills he needed either no help at all or all he could get.

"A man got hurt on the Scrambler last night," Bill disclosed. "Hurt bad I hear. His pod opened and he fell on the concrete pad. Sweep ran over him. Damn near killed him. And they got it all on film."

"No shit," Mudflap whispered, shaking his head sadly.

"What I hear," Bill answered. "Damn shame."

"Poor maintenance."

Burkewood Fun Park was a family-owned amusement park that opened in 1950 and somehow managed – despite its best efforts – to always avoid a buy-out from one of the large theme park conglomerates, such as Marriott, Top Value Enterprises, Taft or Busch. Many claimed to see representatives from those companies touring the park throughout the 1970s, but they always took a pass. Apparently, they didn't see the park as a viable property.

Burkewood however, pretended to be like those mega-parks by operating similarly. Taking a cue from Disney, it was divided into six separate themed areas: Frontier Village, which contained old South and wild west-style rides and shows, like the Scrambler, the flume, a water rapids ride and the Gator wood coaster. The park's main restaurant, the Tennessee Kitchen, was located there.

Adventure Land contained a Spider ride, a Ghost River haunted boat ride, the Steel Phantom coaster and some walk-thru attractions. It also featured a Broadway revue-style live show during full-time operation.

Plaza Americana had more traditional and retro style rides, like the Tilt-a-Whirl, the Wave Swinger, Carousel and Bump'em Cars. Rides that appealed to older parents who had been dragged there with their kids.

The World of Tomorrow was a work in progress, with only a Sky Ride, and a motion theater showing a movie called "Voyage to Jupiter." For some reason an antique car ride was there.

Nipperville was a kid's area, with several clunky old second-hand Coney rides that beeped, farted, swung and drifted in circles. It also featured a puppet show and a newly-installed monkey cage.

Splash Valley was a small water park, with a wave pool, a tube slide and some kiddie slides. Splash Valley, however, was not scheduled to open until Memorial Day, when the park was open full-time. Beside Splash Valley was a man-made body of water called Ford Lake. It hosted a paddleboat ride and a water-skiing show July through August.

"What rides do you guys work on?" I asked.

"We're in Merv's crew and we got priority rides," Bill replied with an air of arrogance. Their rides were more important than anyone else's apparently. "We have the Looper and everything in Adventureland and the World of tomorrow."

"What's the Looper?"

"The steel coaster. Steel Phantom or whatever they're calling it this year," he continued. "I don't think it'll run today."

"Why not?"

"In this weather it won't run consistent speeds. It always gets a set-up. It's a German ride, and German rides don't work in the rain. It must never rain in Germany."

"German rides are shit," Mudflap interrupted. "Now the Japanese build great rides."

Mudflap pushed that sandwich a little further away before continuing. "Damn that sandwich. Walter's crew, the one you're in, has everything in Frontier Village, and Americana, along with the Gator."

"Low priority rides," Bill smirked to Mudflap. "The Swiss and Austrians make damn good rides."

"Hah, yea, all Walter's rides got somebody hurt or killed," Mudflap laughed. "Old Coney, parking lot carnival rides. Rust is the only thing holding them together."

"Whose sandwich is that, anyway?" I asked.

"Walter's – he said he was coming back for it and for nobody to touch it," Bill admitted. "Two minutes later he had forgot about it. That was last Saturday. It can rot there before I touch it. I threw his week-old lunch away one time he got half-shitty with me."

"What do you guys think of the Gator," I inquired. These guys seemed far more responsible than Barnyard or Lump.

"Rickety pile of salt-treated scrap lumber," Bill answered without smiling. I was sure a man of his radius hadn't ridden it in years. "I rode it years ago then later I couldn't pee. I think it gave me a kidney stone."

"It is one rough son of a bitch," Mudflap added, shaking his head sadly. "I rode it last weekend after lubing the wheels and it hung up on the back curve. Shakes me to death. Poor maintenance is what it is."

"After it hung up?" I asked. "What do you mean it hung up?"

"Oh yea," Bill retorted, "every year during winter maintenance the wheels are rebuilt and packed with new grease. We have to run the train for like three days to loosen her up. It always hangs up on the back curve the first few times. We all got to go down there and push it up and around the back curve. It's okay after that."

"I jumped in and rode that last circuit," Mudflap admitted. "I'm sorry I did. My back still hurts."

"Told ya not to."

"Poor maintenance is what it is."

"Damn shame."

A toilet flushed from inside the bathroom and Barnyard finally came out without washing his hands. He rummaged through the fridge and took out a brown bag with a grease stain on the bottom. "Holy Moly there Andy!" He blurted to the three of us as he sat down. He subjected everybody to the same tired Amos 'n Andy rap.

"I don't know if I feel like eating another snack or not," Mudflap wondered out loud, fumbling with his empty nabs wrapper.

Barnyard grabbed his crotch. "I got your snack right here, swingin'."

Mudflap didn't blink. "If you wash your face you can kiss my ass."

"Eat me. There's your snack. *Snock*."

"I'll hit you so hard when you wake up your clothes will be out of style."

"You heard anything on the condition of that guy hurt on the Scrambler?" Bill asked Barnyard, interrupting his potty mouth jousting with Mudflap.

"Not a thing, 10-till-2."

Mudflap laughed.

I looked in confusion at the clock, then back at Bill. He was glaring at Barnyard. "Watch your mouth," he hissed.

What was this all about? "What's 10-till-2?" I asked.

Barnyard started shuffling again. "Didn't they tell you Bill's nickname? 10-till-2?"

I looked at Bill. "Why do they call you 10-till-2?"

Bill angrily shook his head, like I wasn't supposed to be talking about it. "Don't go there."

At that time a young, stupid-looking kid wandered into the lunch room and stood staring at us. His name tag read Josh. He had a weird toothy smile and squinting eyes behind thick glasses. His pants pockets were bulging and soaking wet, like he had fully-loaded, leaking water balloons in each one.

"There you guys are," he announced in the irritating nasal voice of the least popular kid in high school. Josh was a seasonal kid, like me, hired to help Mudflap and Bill.

I was in exclusive company.

"Shoot Josh, we try leaving you but you keep finding us," Bill (or 10-till-2) countered with a little too much sincerity. "Did you finish checking those flume boats?"

Barnyard added his two cents. "*Snock.*"

"Yea, I got them," Josh replied as he turned to me and sat down. "Hey I'm Josh."

I nodded. "Hi Josh, I'm Dale."

"Did you just start today?" he asked.

"Yea."

"I started three weeks ago." This nasal weenie had seniority on me. "I helped the millwrights weld pipe rails on the Ghost River," he continued of his experience. "I know the rides pretty well now. I can check most of them on my own."

"Shoot Josh I can't trust you to inspect my lunch bucket," Mudflap exclaimed as Bill erupted in sarcastic laughter. "Tell him what happened last week during operator training – the drive chain fell off the flume low lift and was laying in the grass. Josh walked right by it. People sitting on the busted lift looking around. Josh just waved at them."

Josh grinned sheepishly then lowered his head. "Why are your pockets so wet," I asked, looking down at his sagging, dripping pants pockets.

"Check this out." Josh stood and walked over to another table, dug both hands in his pants and pulled out huge handfuls of wet, discolored change – mostly dimes, nickels and pennies, with a few quarters thrown in. He dumped both handfuls on the table with a loud clatter. Coins rolled everywhere. He smiled stupidly at us.

"Jesus H Christ!" Mudflap yelled as Bill struggled to his feet, muttered rooty patootie or something and trotted out of the break room. Barnyard blurted a curse and also quickly exited, leaving a confused me, a clueless Josh, a disintegrating sandwich and a really angry Mudflap.

"You know snooping will get your ass fired!" Mudflap yelled at Josh. "Where'd you get that damn money anyhow?"

"It was in the log ride reservoir," Josh whimpered, staring at his ill-gotten pile of change.

"You were snooping when you should have been checking boats!"

"No, I finished checking the boats," Josh explained. "I picked up the money when I was done."

Mudflap just got angrier. "Take it back before Dink or Hutton sees it and fires all of us! And don't do it again!"

Josh raked all four pounds of change back into his pockets and limped out of the shop, his lower lip quivering.

"That dumb little SOB," Mudflap ranted as Josh trudged out the big door into the pouring rain to the imaginary strains of the Peanuts sad piano music. "I told him – and I'll tell you right now," he added, pointing at me for emphasis, "picking up money around a ride will get you fired, no questions asked. If you see money on the ground, even if it's a hundred-dollar bill, leave it the hell alone."

I thought of Barnyard prying through the Gator seats looking for money. It was all I saw him do down there. Apparently, he didn't get that memo. "Will do," I promised.

"Josh is a regular Thomas Edison," Mudflap muttered as he and I left the break room.

We walked back into the drafty maintenance shop. Bill was leaning in the tool cage window, chatting with Tex, free and clear of Josh's wet riches that he was ordered to dump back into the drink. Barnyard was rooting through his tool cabinet.

Another cold wet truck drove into the shop and parked right beside ours. It was Lump.

He got out, also soaking wet. He slammed the door and walked over to his tool cabinet right beside Barnyard, who was still busy digging for something. Lump laid a clipboard with an inspection sheet on the workbench when suddenly Barnyard rose up and grabbed both of Lump's nipples through his wet work shirt and gave them several hard twists right and left.

"Ow! Ow! Ow you bastard!" Lump shrieked in surprised agony as Barnyard hunkered down and seemingly twisted his nipples almost completely off his chest. Laughing, he let go and took off sprinting across the shop, his rotten duct-taped shoes slap-slapping on the cement floor.

Lump was in too much agony to pursue him. "Son of a bitch," he moaned to me, holding his nipples like a stripper trying to keep her pasties from falling off. "My titties stay black and blue all the time because of that punk."

"So I've heard."

Over at the crib window, Bill and Tex were laughing at Lump's black and blue titties. Even Mudflap – fresh from dressing down Josh – had to laugh. I also managed a new-guy smile at Lump's reaction. Barnyard laughed uproariously in relative safety over by a junk pile.

"I'm gonna get your ass," Lump threatened, still in misery. "I can't wait until I fucking retire from this place so I can get away from Barnyard."

"Then you'll be like Bob the guy with the snake on his face," Mudflap retorted as he and Lump approached the tool cage window.

I couldn't let that comment go. "Okay, who or what is Bob the guy with the snake on his face?"

"He was bad news," Tex remarked like it was a dirty secret.

"He worked in building maintenance from the day the park opened until around 1975," Mudflap continued. "A know-it-all. All he had was work – no family or friends. Ugly as sin – his head was a blizzard of dandruff. When he retired, we heard he just sat around his un-air-conditioned house all day in his drawers with a gun in his mouth, daring himself to pull the trigger."

Oh my God.

"Then one day he shows up, buck naked, with that gun in his hand," Lump chimed in. "The barrel was rusty from the hours and hours it spent in his mouth."

"Did he shoot anybody?" I asked, scared to hear the answer.

"Just himself," Lump went on. "I guess being back at work gave him the nerve. Blew his brains out in the fiberglass shop break room. Square-head witnessed it and had to go on disability for post-traumatic stress or something."

"Everybody who retired from here either went crazy or died soon after," Bill revealed. "This is a terrible place to retire from. Bob the guy with the snake on his face went nuts and shot himself. And remember Grambler? In the paint shop? The weekend after his retirement party he squatted to pick up a bundle of tomato stakes at Lowes and his guts exploded. Our previous VP of group sales eleven hours after retiring got killed in a bathroom plumbing accident at home. I'll quit from here before I retire."

"Three to 5-2, *scratch*."

"Mudflap answer your radio," Tex bellowed. Startled, Mudflap grabbed his radio from his hip holster.

"Jeez Tex, I'm right beside you. 5-2 go ahead." While Mudflap answered his radio, I saw Josh out the big shop door disappearing through the rain across the shop parking lot to put his money back in the Flume reservoir. I never saw someone so beaten. He looked like his butt was wiping out his foot prints as he walked.

I overheard Mudflap's radio call. "You got anybody available you can send down to the Spider," somebody asked. "They got a couple of broken bucket springs. *Scratch*."

Mudflap thought a minute. "10-4. I'll bring the newbie down. 5-2 clear."

He holstered his radio and pointed to me. "Come on young man, you're going to get a lesson in replacing Spider springs. You got any tools?"

"No. But I was supposed to see someone named Judy for my orientation."

"Screw that," Mudflap dismissed my concerns. "All she's going to tell you is don't pick up money and don't do anything stupid. She's cute though. Alright, all you need is a ratchet and a one-half-inch deep well socket. I got one."

Barnyard appeared safe from Lump and walked over to the tool cage window beside Bill as I walked over and got in Mudflap's truck.

"What's up, 10-till-2!"

Chapter 5: in which I get an easy lesson on changing Spider springs and a hard lesson in accepting offers to ride

THE RAIN STOPPED and the sun was actually trying to peek through the dense fast-moving cloud cover when Mudflap pulled out of his parking space in yet another of those white trucks with me riding shotgun. He popped in a stick of cinnamon gum without asking if I wanted a piece.

"Why did they call him Bob the guy with the snake on his face?" I asked. I had so many questions.

"A snake tattoo," Mudflap explained. "It rose up out of his shirt collar, wrapped around his neck around and over his ear. Weird as shit. He said an artist in Hawaii did it after the war."

I tried to imagine such a thing. Mudflap then broke my train of thought.

"You know we still have a Spider ride, even though they were banned in North Dakota."

I was curious. "Why are they banned in North Dakota?"

"The arms kept breaking, throwing the buckets onto the ground. Injured a couple people at a state fair there. The manufacturer put out a gusset kit to beef it up, but North Dakota said screw a gusset kit and banned the whole ride."

"Does this park have the gusset kit?"

"And then some," Mudflap laughed. "We welded enough steel on that ride to make a second ride."

Mudflap stomped the gas and drove so fast through a narrow gate near the closed employee cafeteria that I instinctively drew in my shoulders. We emerged in Frontier Village just past the antique car ride.

"One time we had a park-wide power failure and the antique cars was the only ride open," he informed me as we passed the station with numerous small-scale Model-T Fords waiting for riders. "The line stretched all the way to Doo-Doo's Crap Shack or whatever they called it then."

After passing the car ride, we entered into the Americana area. A guy waved us to a stop beside the old Carousel.

Mudflap pulled over under the Carousel canopy. A painted cherub up on the fascia smiled down at us. This Carousel dated back to the early 1910s, and retained much of its gilded-era charm. Mudflap rolled down his window and the guy walked up to it and stuck his head a little too far into the window.

"Any of you seen battle?"

"I never went to Vietnam," Mudflap replied, leaning away from the guy's head.

"No, Phil Battle. The welder. I was supposed to meet him down here at 6:00 a.m."

Another unreliable employee, keeping someone waiting.

"He's supposed to be welding braces in the center mast tube on the Wave Swinger," the guy continued. "I have the braces in my truck. I've been waiting three hours. I ain't got all day."

The guy's alcohol-soaked breath filled the cab of the truck like a bad dream. "I don't know what the hell you're talking about," Mudflap admitted. "But goddamn you need a breath mint."

He rolled up his window and drove off, leaving the inebriated contractor standing under the canopy, confused, with no Battle.

"Damn that guy's breath," Mudflap exclaimed, waving his hand in front of his face. "I got a mouthful of it."

"Okay, what about the nickname 10-till-2?" I asked.

Mudflap snickered. "When Bill walks or stands, his feet point out at an angle. One day he and I were standing at the workbench and I looked down at something. His feet said it was 10-till-2. He's real touchy about it. That, spending money and fresh haircuts."

We eventually stopped in front of a ride that looked like a big black widow spider with four orange buckets on the end of four arms. We got out and Mudflap went around the truck, dropped the tailgate and retrieved a ratchet, a deep-well socket and two screwdrivers from his toolbox.

"Holy moly there Andy!"

I looked up and saw Barnyard driving by us real slow in the opposite direction, his window down. He appeared to have nothing to do.

"You got no rides in this area, get your chicken lips out of here," Mudflap ordered.

"I'll go where I want there, Andy."

"Go down to the Carousel and pick up that drunk contractor."

"Oh, I've been looking for him, he's got the Wave Swinger braces," Barnyard blurted before gunning his truck and driving away down the empty midway. Flags on the buildings and rides fluttered madly in the cold morning wind.

Mudflap turned toward me. "That Barnyard will get on your freaking nerves after a while."

He was on my nerves before I even met him.

I dutifully followed Mudflap through the exit gate surrounding the ride and walked over to the closest bucket that had a trash bag tied off on the lap bar. Trash bags serve multiple uses in the amusement industry.

"There's a big black spring under the hinge on these buckets that assist in opening and especially closing for loading and unloading," Mudflap explained. He sat on the pad under the tied-off bucket and motioned for me to do the same. "See here."

I sat down and looked up through a small opening. A large black spring was dangling flaccidly from an eyebolt in the footrest side.

"When that spring breaks, it's too hard for the operator to open and close the bucket," Mudflap instructed as he put his ratchet on a jam nut on the back of the eyebolt and loosened it after lifting the broken spring out of the foot rest side. "Go over to the operator's panel, you'll see some new springs. Grab one and bring it over."

I got up, walked over to the panel and saw a stack of six springs under the operator's console. I picked one and carried it back.

"Get down here I'll show you how it goes on – then you can do the next one while I check the other buckets." He hooked the new spring on the foot rest side eyebolt then grunted and hooked it on the other eyebolt. He tightened up the jam nut, drawing the eyebolt in and forcing some pressure on the spring.

"All set." We got up and he unlatched and opened the bucket. "See how easy it opens now." I held it and snapped it shut. Easy. "Sometimes you need a screwdriver to pry off the broken spring, so take it and the ratchet over yonder and fix the other one while I give the ride a once over."

Confident in my new spring-changing skills I sat down under the other bucket on the opposite side of the ride, looking up through the hole. Sure enough the spring, like the last one, swung uselessly from one of the eyebolts. I got your snack swinging, I thought, as I loosened the jam nut just like Mudflap had done. A new spring suddenly landed beside me with a clatter. "You're going to need that."

I had some trouble lifting the old one off, but a little prying with the screwdriver finally released it. "If you get really good at that you can change them between cycles when the ride is running," Mudflap yelled as I looked up and saw him jam another screwdriver between the fiberglass bucket and seat cushion, looking for money. He wasn't taking his own advice. "It's a lot like a NASCAR pit stop," he continued as he forced his hand behind the cushion. "The ride stops, you run in, change the spring then load the bucket and off she goes with no down time."

I know why Josh and I got the stern "no picking up money" speech from Mudflap – we were encroaching on his territory.

I hooked the new spring on the one eyebolt but had to really shove to hook it on the other side. I wrapped my right hand around the spring and shoved it hard, but missed the other eye and the spring snapped shut, pinching the meat between my thumb and forefinger.

"Ow dammit!"

"What the hell!" Mudflap laughed from one of the buckets. "You didn't pinch your hand, did you?"

"Yes."

"Hah! Those springs are strong. They'll nip a fingertip right off if you're not careful. Just ask Lump."

I rubbed my freezing and now pinched hand and loosened the eyebolt as far as it would go. This time the spring slipped right over. I tightened the spring back up, gathered the tools and stood up, joining Mudflap over at the operator's console, satisfied with my job but angry about my now-blood blistered hand.

"How's the hand," he asked.

"Hurts like hell." I was terrified I was earning a nickname, so I just shut up.

Mudflap inserted a key in the console and turned it, starting a motor and pump in the center of the ride. "All I got to do now is cycle the ride and sign the sheet." I noticed he was wearing a watch he did not have on earlier. He must have found it in one of the seats. "You ever ridden this ride?"

"Years ago."

"You wanna ride?"

I thought this was a cool opportunity, and a perk to working there – unlimited rides, without waiting in line, all by yourself. It's like being a rich kid whose daddy rented the entire park just for you.

"Hell yea, I'll ride!"

Mudflap walked out, unlatched a bucket, laid it down and let me climb in. Once in he raised and snapped it shut. The spring made it easy. I buckled the seatbelt and waited, a big doofus grin on my face. Oh boy, this was going to be great. I never rode a ride by myself before. I was a pig in slop.

I heard the rotation motor start. "Welcome to the Spider," Mudflap spieled. "Keep your arms and legs inside the bucket at all times. Enjoy your ride ... you dumbass."

What? Why did he call me a dumbass?

"You know this is one of the only rides in the whole park not on a timer," Mudflap announced over the PA as the green go light came on and he pulled back on a joystick on the panel. The ride slowly started rotating. "You're going to wish it was on a timer."

Once the ride was up to rotation speed he pulled back on the other joystick and the arms started raising and lowering in sequence as they rotated. At this point I noticed something was different – the ride was rotating counter-clockwise, which was backwards from how it usually operated. It was uncomfortable and unnatural.

As I swooped and rotated, I saw Mudflap stretch a bungee cord around the joysticks, hooking them on the edge of the console, holding the controls in the "on" position. He walked away from the panel, smiling at me.

"I'll be back in about fifteen minutes," he yelled as I blew past him counterclockwise. "I got an appointment in the Adventureland bathroom. My breakfast burrito is fixing to say *hasta la vista*."

Fifteen minutes? I had been on the ride fifteen seconds and already I was getting sick.

That bastard tricked me. He got in his truck and drove off, leaving me alone on this Godforsaken ride. Suddenly I was in a spinning and swooping torture device right out of a Wes Craven movie with no way off. Unhooking the seatbelt and jumping out would get me killed.

Around and around I went, spinning, dipping suddenly up then down, getting sicker and dizzier at each rotation. I closed my eyes but that made it worse. I loved this ride when it ran two minutes clockwise like normal. I couldn't believe Mudflap did this to me, he seemed so friendly, so ordinary.

Was this a rite of initiation? Something they did to the new guys to keep them from ever getting on a ride again?

After what seemed like several minutes or several days, I caught a fleeting glimpse of somebody standing beside a truck. On the next pass I could tell they were grinning at me. On the next pass I saw it was Barnyard.

"Do you want off?" He yelled as I passed him again. I could only nod my head. I felt like killing myself.

"I didn't hear you."

I jerked around to face him as my arm swooped down within about twelve feet in front of him. I looked him straight in the eye. "Get me off this fucking ride!" I screamed as I shot past him. I swooped back up and spun again, leaving the pit of my stomach somewhere on the ground.

Barnyard took his sweet time walking to the operator's console. He unhooked the bungee cord, then slowly returned the joysticks back to neutral load position. The ride slowed to a stop ... almost.

"One more time?"

I was delirious. "No God no ..."

Barnyard sadistically shoved the handles backward and the ride came roaring back to life, swooping and swinging me, up and down, only in the opposite direction this time. The sudden change of direction almost made me black out. I tried to jump out but I was too disoriented to unbuckle my seat belt.

"Ha ha ha ha ha!" Barnyard cackled as he quickly returned the handles to the neutral position. "You were going in reverse. That was forward. Consider that chocolate cake and ice cream."

Once the ride stopped and Barnyard lowered my bucket to the ground, I unhooked my seat belt, clamored over the bucket, then fell lifelessly onto the ground. Good thing my stomach was empty.

Barnyard thought my predicament was hilarious as I lay there on that wet pavement, trying to focus. "Guess you won't be getting' on any more rides," he shouted with glee. "Holy moly there Andy! I think I say I think I'm gonna be sick!"

After a minute or so I was able to get up and stagger over to Barnyard's truck, swimming in misery. "I'm going to kill Mudflap," I groaned as I laid face down across the cold hood, which felt good against my face. "He left me on that ride for fifteen minutes."

"You weren't on there fifteen minutes," Barnyard informed me. "I was watching – you were on there about six minutes at most. You'd be dead after fifteen minutes. That or turned wrong-side out."

"I'm still going to kill Mudflap."

"Let it go," Barnyard warned. "Consider it a lesson learned. Everybody's been there. This son of a bitch used to work here, his name was Frank Fumes. He got me inside a ride called the Time Traveler the same way. 'You inspect the inside,' he said. Stupid me, I got in and he closed the door. It was a drum that spun you real fast then the floor dropped down. I was stuck to the wall of the drum as it spun around. Frank left me in there so long the ride overheated. It was down all day after that. I had to go to the emergency room with a blood clot right behind my eye. Made my eye bulge out like a ping-pong ball. Frank was fired after they found out what he did."

I looked up at him. "Seriously?"

"Yep. Another guy rode the Gator coaster fifty-seven times in a row before they let him out. Blew him through the station without even slowing down. He shit all over the car and his legs were useless for an hour. He went home and never came back. Wally in the carpenter shop rode a kiddie swinging ship ride for thirty minutes once. He was passed out the last five minutes, swaying' back and forth like a dead man."

"4-0 to 3-6, *scratch*."

Barnyard apparently turned his radio back on. He pulled it from his holster.

"3-6 go ahead."

"Go see if they need a hand at the rapids ride with that gearbox, *scratch*."

"10-4." He holstered the radio. "Fuck. I knew I shouldn't have answered."

"What's wrong," I asked, my head back down on the hood.

"They're over at the white-water rapids ride pulling off a gearbox that broke down during a test run yesterday. It's frozen on the drive drum shaft and they're having a hell of a time getting it off. So much for another break."

I rose up and poured myself into Barnyard's truck. "I was supposed to see someone named Judy this morning."

"Shit, all she will do is tell you don't pick up money and don't do anything stupid. Her orientation is a joke." *Snock*.

We rode back through Americana. In my stupor I failed to notice the drunken contractor, or any of the rides or the shops or the games coming to life as the operators began showing up to begin the first day of this, the 1980 season of Burkewood Fun Park.

Chapter 6: in which I witness a spectacularly botched repair and almost make sausage of a co-worker

BARNYARD DROVE BACK on a service road before turning onto a gravel drive that wound through the woods and ended at the White Water Rapids ride station.

A three-year-old ride in the Frontier Village section, White Water Rapids was a particularly ambitious attraction that featured rafts that carried six guests at a time through a rapid white-water trough, generated by water pumped by three huge pumps from a million-gallon reservoir. The ride was very popular in hot weather, but since the weather was so terrible it was probably a good day to keep it down to fix it.

I thought about that Time Traveler ride Barnyard mentioned earlier because I rode it when I was twelve, trying to impress some girls from my church youth group. "Hey, whatever happened to the Time Traveler," I asked Barnyard. "I noticed they took it out a few years ago."

"Vomit-induced corrosion they called it," Barnyard replied. "Remember how people used to puke the minute they got off right there at the exit? It got so bad they put a water hose there for an operator whose only job was to wash the puke off the exit. After ten years of Voban powder and that puke-filled water running down the legs under the ride, they corroded so bad they couldn't be fixed. They just took the ride out. Good riddance I say."

"Speaking of puking," Barnyard added, "I was supposed to take that contractor over to the Wave Swinger, but he was throwing up in the bushes behind the Carousel. *Snock.*"

A good contractor is hard to find.

Barnyard and I got out of the truck and walked up the white-water station exit ramp then down the other side, hopped an old-fashioned decorative split rail fence and walked down by the three conveyor belts that transported the boats from the end of the ride up to the station. I was still pretty queasy from my Spider ride but was getting over it.

Bill, an electrician named Mac and a short, heavyset guy with a remarkable comb-over in a cheap, plastic-looking clip-on tie stood by the drive unit to the middle conveyor. A complex, homemade steel jig was welded to the gearbox, and a hundred-ton hydraulic ram was set in the jig. It was connected to a hydraulic pump that hummed loudly. Another torture device.

"What's going on," Barnyard asked.

Bill looked at him then at me. "I thought we were getting some real help," he snickered, winking at me. "We got the electric motor off okay but the gearbox is galled to the shaft and won't come off. It's a press fit and won't budge. We got a hundred tons of pressure on it and it just sits there."

I skillfully glanced down at Bill's feet. Sure enough, they indicated it was 10-till-2. The guys were correct.

"You know what we need," the short comb-over guy in the plastic tie chimed in, "we need heat on the gear box sleeve to expand it. And we need Freon to freeze and shrink that shaft." He picked up the button for the hydraulic ram and pushed it, watching the dial indicator. The pressure went into the red as the electric motor screamed. It was maxed out. He released the button.

"I'm scared that son of a bitch is going to ..."

BANG! All our chests jumped as something suddenly broke loose. The pressure indicator plummeted to zero.

The plastic tie guy seemed happy. "Now we're getting somewhere."

"Rooty patootie," Bill chirped, happy that something seemed to be happening. Maybe the gearbox was coming off the shaft. The guy in the plastic tie pressed the button again, running the pressure again into the red. I stepped back as something groaned. It did not seem right.

BANG again. Black oil spewed and started pouring in a splashing stream down into the reservoir.

"OIL!" the man in the plastic tie yelled, "somebody get a bucket and catch it!" Bill and Barnyard scrambled in a circle looking for something to catch the oil before it fouled the entire ride water supply. Barnyard found an old empty tar bucket under the station and thrust it under the spewing gearbox, which had cracked in half and was blowing gallons of dirty oil. He caught about a pint. The other six gallons burbled down into the reservoir water. All the pressure bled off the hydraulic ram, and everything died, especially hope.

"You guys were supposed to drain the oil out of that that damn gearbox," the plastic tie guy shouted.

Suddenly half of the massive gearbox housing broke off with a sickening crunch, knocking Barnyard's bucket out of his hand. Busted housing, an assortment of gears and pins and a tar bucket half full of black oil tumbled and dropped about twenty feet down into the reservoir with a huge greasy splash.

"Catch that damn thing!" the man in the plastic tie yelled, which was ill-advised because the gearbox weighed over 250 pounds and was already at the bottom of the reservoir under 10 feet of water. A rainbow instantly bubbled to the surface.

"No God no," the man in the tie moaned as Bill, Barnyard and I looked forlornly at the bubbling and polluted million gallons of water, which was going to have to be drained and replaced at a huge cost. The electrician lit a cigarette and smiled sadly.

"I'll call the plumbers," he pre-emptively offered.

The guy in the plastic tie stomped away, seemingly furious that not one of us would sacrifice our lives by diving between that massive falling gearbox and the ride's water supply. "That was Dink," Barnyard informed me. "He's got to go back and tell his boss, Byram, that we have to pump out the ride into trucks and scrub the reservoir, plus spend a couple days waiting on a new gearbox."

"Why do we have to pump the water into trucks?" I asked.

"The drain system for the ride reservoir leads eventually to the York River. The plumbers test the water and if the water passes it can be pumped into the river. But if it gets polluted, like it is now, it has to be pumped into tanker trucks and taken to a purification plant. Costs a freaking fortune apparently. The park had to pay giant fines a few years ago for dumping car batteries, used motor oil and tires on the ground for fifteen years. Now they're real buttholes about pollution."

"Rooty patootie. Time to get the torches and plasma cutter," Bill commented as he waddled off. His plan apparently was to simply burn off the rest of the gearbox still stuck on the conveyor drive drum shaft. Dink was up in the station barking into the telephone.

The electrician looked at his watch, bored. He had no dog in this hunt.

Dink stomped back down the station steps over to the shattered gearbox. He looked resigned. "Byram said to start the pumps to lower the reservoir," he suggested. "Tex is going to drive the boom truck over to lift the busted box out when the level is down. Then we'll reverse the pumps and pump all the water out of the reservoir to clean it. I have to find five or six available county tank trucks. He's mad as hell about this, it's going to cost thousands of dollars. Wear your reservoir-cleaning clothes the rest of the week."

Barnyard volunteered to start the pumps. I followed him as he clipped his key lanyard off a belt loop and walked up into the station to the operator's panel. He keyed in the power, then he walked over to a button mounted in a box on the side of a shed while I waited in the station. He then keyed another switch, which sounded an ear-splitting five-second alarm. He waited a second then pushed a large red button.

Directly below me under the exit ramp three huge 100-horsepower pumps roared to life, instantly pulling thousands of gallons of oil-contaminated water through their impellors into the ride, creating an almost instant whitewater river. It was breathtaking to watch as weir boards bolted to the floor of the cement trough created fast waves and whitecaps all the way to the last holding area before the lift to the station. It took less than fifteen seconds for the ride to fill with rushing, but polluted water.

Barnyard walked back over and stood beside me, watching the water fill the ride.

"I'd like to body surf through there," I observed.

"The boards would tear you to pieces," he replied in a Captain Buzzkill kind of way. "They had a guy take a kayak down through there a couple years ago for a commercial. His canoe hit one of the weir boards and flipped. He tumbled down through the ride, beating off the boards and sides of the trough. When they finally fished him out, he was beat to shit. He said it was the worst thing he had ever done."

Forget it then. The water line on the reservoir wall indicated the level had dropped about eighteen inches already.

We walked down the exit stairs, climbed the fence and walked back over to the busted belt. Dink was standing with one foot on the side of the mammoth reservoir, watching the water level drop as the huge pumps sent more water through the ride. I stopped and stood next to him for a minute before he suddenly looked up at me.

"Who are you?" he grunted.

"I'm Dale. I just started today."

"Who hired you?"

"Walter Baxter."

"Why?"

"Why did Walter hire me?"

"Yes."

How do you answer that? "Um, I guess because he thought I would be a good addition to the team?"

"You cannot tell anybody about this," he ordered in a not too subtle way.

"About getting hired?"

"No."

"You mean about the oil in the water?"

"Yep. The EPA will crucify us."

"Okay."

"Have you seen Judy for your orientation?"

"Not yet, but I will."

Dink pointed into the reservoir. "Eventually the water level will drop then equalize," he instructed. "Tex needs to get that truck over here right away so we can get the gearbox out while the level is at its lowest. Where the hell is he?"

"I don't know."

"Damn!" Dink covered his face and bent way over, then stood back up. "I just realized we're pumping oil-contaminated water through the entire ride," he blurted. "We'll have to steam-clean out not just the reservoir but the entire trough. Shit!"

The electrician ground his cigarette out on the sole of his shoe. His nametag read Mac. His radio was squawking something about checking somebody in holding lake 2, whatever that meant.

Dink caught part of the transmission and suddenly yanked out his radio. "4-0 to 3," he barked.

"3 go ahead, *scratch*."

"10-9 that last call."

"I said I had a seasonal guy working over in Lake 2 at the rapids ride but now I hear the water is in the ride, *scratch*."

"Yea, we have the pumps on to bring the reservoir level down to pump it out."

"Somebody better check on Josh in Lake 2 then, *scratch*."

"10-4."

Dink turned to me. "You know where Lake 2 is?"

I had a rough idea. "Through these woods at the other side of the cave, right?"

"Yea, walk over there and make sure we didn't drown that dumbass."

I walked through the woods surrounding the ride over to Lake 2. Holding lake 2 was the informal name of what was simply a holding area with an air-powered gate. When several boats got into the holding area, they were channeled into single file by fence posts wrapped decoratively with ship lashing. An operator in a small tower opened the gate to let one boat out at a time for their final leg through a man-made cave just before the lift belts. It was designed to keep proper spacing between boats.

I got to Lake 2, which was completely filled with rushing water. Seated on top of one of those fence posts, surrounded by deep, boiling water was my fellow seasonal employee Josh. He was soaking wet from his chest to his shoes and shivering.

We stared at each other for just a beat. "What the hell were you doing?" I asked.

"I was replacing rusted bolts in the gates when the water suddenly came. It almost washed me away."

"Didn't you hear the alarm?"

"What alarm?"

"The alarm that goes off when they turn on the pumps. It's your signal to get out."

"I heard something. I thought it was the lunch whistle."

"Are you kidding?"

I stared at Josh as he looked at me for a minute, trying to form words. "Well how am I going to get off this post," he finally asked.

Josh truly was a Thomas Edison. "They need to pump down the reservoir so they can get a boom in and take out a gearbox that fell in the water," I told him. "You might have to sit there until they're done."

"That might take an hour or longer," he complained. "I can't sit here an hour. I'm about to fall off now. My ass is asleep."

It was my first day. How was I supposed to grasp this? "I don't know what to tell you."

Josh looked around. He was in a pretty difficult predicament. The water was getting deeper and faster. "Find a board or something that will stretch from the concrete trough over here that I can walk across," he finally suggested.

It was over twelve feet from Josh's post to the cement wall. "That's a stupid idea," I retorted. "The board could break."

"But I don't really have no other choices. You gotta find something!"

I had to admit that soaked dumbass was right. I walked around between Lake 2 and the cave, finding a pile of scraps left over from construction. I finally located a half-rotted, concrete-encrusted fourteen-foot long 2x4, which I dragged back to the lake.

"This is the best I could find."

"Hurry up and lay it across, the water's getting' deeper and my ass hurts," Josh ordered. "All my tools are in the bottom of the lake."

I laid the 2x4 down and slid it out to Josh's post. It was further away than I thought, and I almost lost it when the end dipped down into the rushing water, but it finally reached him. He grabbed his end and laid it on a flat brace beside his perch. I laid my end on the cement wall with only an inch to spare. The 2x4 was soggy and had a bow in the middle. The water was roaring without mercy by now, over Josh's brand-new Red Wing steel-toe work boots.

Josh scooched around and gently put one foot on the board. It was showtime – a death-defying, fourteen-foot tightrope walk on a 3-1/2" wide board, over raging, frigid, white water rapids.

"I don't think this is very safe," Josh murmured, watching the water level rise even higher. It was almost to the top of his post, and only an inch below the 2X4. He was starting to freak a little bit.

He put his other foot on the tightrope and, holding his hand on his post for support, slowly rose to a standing position. The board creaked. The roaring water splashed against the post, sending splash plumes ten feet in the air. It was getting scary.

Suddenly, on the other side of the lake, a giant sheet of aluminum mounted on the wall roared to life and started swinging back and forth. It was called the wavemaker, and it triggered automatically when the water reached operating depth. This churned the raging water up even more. Lake 2 was apocalyptic, watery chaos. Several yards away, an automatic air-pressurized geyser suddenly shot a blast of water fifteen feet up, followed a few seconds later by a second one. Josh had to act fast – I knew there were three geysers, and I also knew the last one was in our vicinity.

"Do it quickly," I suggested. "Hop hop hop you're done. By the way, can you swim?"

"Okay." Josh went one ... two ... thr ... then the third geyser unfortunately right underneath blasted him and the board into the raging water.

I watched in horror as Josh was quickly swept away. I saw his head only briefly when it banged against the gate, sending his glasses into the roiling rapids before he entered the dark cave about fifty feet away. I prayed that once he got through the cave, he would land on the lift conveyor on the other side, where he should be okay.

Then again, if he missed the lift belts he would be swept into the pumps. And he would be like sausage through a grinder. Of course, he could be unconscious from whacking his head and be drowned before either of those scenarios occurred.

Sensing a panic attack, I turned and ran fast through the woods back to the reservoir. I saw Dink standing at the operator's console, talking on the phone as he watched the water level. At the same time a huge boom truck backed slowly to the far edge of the reservoir from the gravel driveway. Mac the electrician was still on the ground lighting another cigarette. Nobody knew about Josh in the water.

I ran past Mac and glanced down at the pumps. The water was low enough to expose a steel grating that filled the bottom of the pump sump. I ran up the steps into the station, my chest about to explode. I had to tell somebody fast about Josh.

"No, we had 100 tons of pressure on it but it shattered the gearbox housing," Dink commented into the phone. He had his back to me. I stopped and paused a second. "Mm, yea, yea," he muttered.

"Dink?"

Without turning he raised a finger, indicating for me to wait. "It will take two days to drain the water and refill it," he instructed to whoever was on the other end. "No. No. We have to code it mechanical downtime."

"Dink? We have kind of a problem ..."

"We should have one down in long-term inventory," he said as he shot me an angry look over his shoulder. "We'll take it oh shit!"

He suddenly dropped the phone when he saw Josh exiting the tunnel, flailing in the turbulent water past the safety of the belts straight toward the pumps. He looked alive, thank God, just terrified and helpless in the fast water.

"There's a man in the water heading for the trash screens!" Dink yelled down to Mac the electrician.

Mac suddenly showed more life than he had since I arrived there as he trotted over to the edge of the reservoir. Just as he peeked over the side, Josh washed like a beached whale up on the trash screen grating down in the sump, gasping for air but basically unhurt from his wild ride.

"How did that son of a bitch get in there?" Dink ordered, before he looked straight at me. "And why didn't you tell me he was in there? Damn you guys!"

He paused. "You cannot tell anyone about this."

I had been working there not even four hours and I had more secrets than the Pope.

Chapter 7: in which I cause a critical employee benefit to magically disappear

THANK GOD JOSH did not get sucked into the pump impellor like sausage through a grinder because the trash screens – that grating I saw earlier when the water level dropped – caught him. After landing on the screens he got up, shook himself off and casually climbed a metal ladder mounted on the concrete wall. Dink met him at the top of the ladder. It was an undramatic ending to a dramatic situation.

"What the hell were you doing in that water?" Dink demanded before turning to me. "And why the hell didn't you tell me? He could have gotten killed in there, and it would have been my ass."

"I was working in Lake 2 and the pumps started and I got stranded on a fence post," Josh confessed.

This Dink guy was starting to piss me off. "I tried to tell you he was in the water but you were on the phone," I objected. "We tried to get Josh out but he fell in ... and ..."

As I rambled on, a terrible snapping, grinding noise suddenly erupted from the far no. 3 pump behind us. The entire station rattled like an earthquake. Shards of shattered 2x4 abruptly sprayed from the pump outlet and the pump shuddered horribly before there was a loud and nauseating metallic cannon report. The pump screamed to a crescendo before it popped and shut down completely. Black smoke poured from the cooling vents. The other pumps continued like nothing happened.

"What the hell now!" Dink shouted. He hustled over to that pump's outlet and looked down from the exit ramp. Splintered remnants of Josh's fourteen-foot long walk board floated in the backwash of the outlet sump.

Mac the electrician came up to where we were standing. Josh was shivering from being soaking wet on a forty-four-degree morning. "There was two chunks of lumber in the water," Mac told Dink. "The trash screen caught one of them but the water level was so low the other one went under the screen and into the pump impellor."

Dink's face bleached white.

"That loud crack was the main seven-inch impellor shaft shearing in half," Mac explained.

"God no."

"I'm afraid so," Mac continued. "I saw the coupling just start spinning crazy after that first loud noise, right before the motor spun out and blew. The shaft is rung off, right at the threaded coupling. And I'm assuming that since that 100-horsepower motor is currently on fire, we'll need a new one."

Dink leaned on the handrail with his face in his hands. "That shaft and impellor is one piece," he groaned. "This alone is a $300,000 repair, without labor. It will take weeks."

He looked at me, resigned. "Take this man back to the break room and get some dry clothes on him," he ordered me like I was Josh's mother. "You guys have caused me enough headaches on this ride."

I was about to protest Dink's baseless accusations when suddenly a shredded article of clothing loudly blew through another pump outlet on the other side. Dink spun to look.

"Now what!"

"That w-w-was my c-c-coat," claimed Josh through chattering teeth. We then watched scraps of his green military-style winter coat – which got yanked from his torso during his journey – wash down the ride, mingling with the scraps of 2x4.

I thought it was a good time to leave anyway before we started getting questioned why that board was even in the water. "C'mon Josh we'll walk back."

"I know a sh-sh-short c-c-cut," he replied.

Josh led me through the woods on a pine needle path. His shoes squished as he walked. We passed the back side of the water flume ride where he had to throw his pocketful of money back. A flume ride is nothing more than a fiberglass trough set on steel stanchions. A lone female operator wrapped in a parka walked absently through the trough, doing one more walk-through before park opening. We came out by the flume pump motor house on asphalt. The maintenance building was right in front of us.

I was curious about Josh's wild ride. "What was it like being washed through that trough?"

"I don't remember m-m-much," he answered. "I hit my h-h-head pretty hard on the Lake 2 gate."

A wave of dread suddenly passed through me. "I hope your tools don't go through one of those other pumps. We'll ruin every pump on that ride."

As we approached the shop, Mudflap, Lump and some guy I had not yet met were standing outside the shop by one of the guy's personal pickup trucks, looking inside the bed. Lump was massaging his black and blue titties. Apparently Barnyard got him again.

"Hey Thomas Edison, you're soaking wet," Mudflap yelled. The other guys looked curiously at us.

"Yea I kind of fell in the white-water ride," Josh admitted, flashing that stupid grin.

"Don't tell them what happened," I implored, "We'll look like idiots."

"Where are your coke bottle glasses?"

"Oh." It just then occurred to Josh that he no longer had his glasses. "Damn I guess they're in the ride," he groaned, feeling his face for the non-existent glasses. We walked over to see what the guys were looking at in the truck bed.

It was a black trash bag. Then it moved. The unknown guy reached in an pulled the bag open.

Christ almighty.

"I've never seen a snapping turtle that big," Mudflap declared.

"Me neither," Lump agreed. "Where'd it come from?"

"I picked it up outta the road on my way to work this morning," admitted the unknown guy. He grinned and I saw his stained teeth were filled with flecks of plug chewing tobacco. I could almost smell his oral cancer.

This turtle was like looking at a living dinosaur. Its moldy shell was at least eighteen inches across. Its head was a fist-size knot, barely recognizable as a face. Its tail was over a foot long.

What you gonna do with him, Nard?" Mudflap asked.

"Man, that thing's good eatin'," Nard, the oral cancer guy responded.

"My God, Nard, you really ain't going to eat that turtle, are you?" Lump protested.

"Hell yea. They're good eatin'."

"That turtle is 100 years old," Mudflap exclaimed. "Look at him – he's got moss on his shell, he's so old. He ain't nothing but gristle. Take him up here in the woods and turn him loose."

"Hell no. They're good eatin'." Nard was insistent.

Josh and I walked away from that preposterous argument that was going nowhere and went into the break room. It was warm in there. A guy almost as sinewy as Nard's turtle, with glasses just as thick as the ones Josh used to own and a cap pulled down to his eyes, sat smoking at one of the tables. Walter's sandwich still sat on the other table. Josh went behind a wall of lockers to change into dry clothes.

"Howdy," the sinewy guy nodded at me.

"Hi."

I poured myself a cup of instant coffee made in the real coffee coffeemaker as Josh changed behind the wall of lockers. I then sat down across from the sinewy smoking guy.

"What was all that activity over yonder at white water," he asked as he ground out his cigarette. His name tag read Chunky, even though he weighed a hundred pounds soaking wet.

"Where do I start," I countered. "We shattered a gear box, polluted a million gallons of water with several gallons of gear oil, almost drowned an employee and destroyed one of the 100-horsepower pumps. And it's barely even breakfast."

"Shit," Chunky laughed, "that's a lot of destruction in one morning. And the Scrambler nearly killed Sir Lawrence Olivier last night."

"What? Sir Lawrence Olivier?"

"One of those actors making those commercials."

Out in the shop I heard one of the mechanic's radios start squawking "code two, code two emergency!" The tool cage phone rang non-stop. Why didn't Tex answer it? Something awful was breaking loose. What the hell?

Bill ran into the break room straight to the instant coffee pot. "Rooty patootie," he mumbled as he quickly poured a cup. He apparently needed coffee before responding to a code 2, whatever that was.

"What's going on out there," Chunky asked Bill.

"Dumbass Tex backed the boom truck too far over the edge of the white-water reservoir and dumped it ass-end down into the water."

Mudflap suddenly stuck his head in the door. "Never mind the code 2, 10-till-2, Tex ain't hurt. But the boom truck is on life support." Life speeded back up to a crawl as Mudflap walked into the break room. "Dink said he's going to have to call one of those wreckers they use to tow airplanes that skid off the tarmacs. He said the white-water ride was going to blow his maintenance budget for the year."

"Hey thanks for leaving me on the Spider, Mudflap."

He looked at me and laughed. "Welcome to the club, new guy. Looks like you came out of it okay."

"I don't have a trauma-induced brain tumor, if that's what you mean by coming out okay."

Chunky stood to leave. "You see that damn turtle Nard found in the road?"

"Yea," Mudflap responded. "He says it's good eatin'."

"Shit that retard don't know nothing, most including how to cook and eat a turtle," Chunky scoffed in a most politically incorrect way, making me wince. "Remember that time the paint shop gave away a whole bunch of half-full cans of left-over paint? Nard got about fifty cans, mixed them all up in one tub at home and painted a shed. A week later he asked us what was the difference between oil and latex. He mixed 'em all up together. What a mess."

Mudflap chuckled. "Well he's under the impression now he's a turtle gourmet."

"It ain't nothing but skin and gristle no how."

"Nard or the turtle?"

Chunky and Mudflap left the break room laughing just as Josh finally came out of the locker area in dry clothes. He had on boot-cut high-water jeans and one of the park-issued grey work shirts that I had not gotten yet.

"That took long enough," I observed. "What were you doing back there?"

Josh grinned. "You know we make like four dollars an hour?"

"Yea?"

"I've been sitting back on the bench for fifteen minutes."

"And?"

"So, the entire time I sat on the bench doing nothing? I made a dollar."

Atta boy Josh. You really stuck it to the man.

As we sat there a tall guy with red hair wearing a starched white shirt and bulbous 1979 knit tie entered the break room. He looked important and was carrying a huge silver deli and fruit tray. There was a massive gold University of Virginia ring on his finger.

"Good morning gentlemen," he stated with much enthusiasm as he set the tray on the break table. "We had a food tray left over from our marketing and group sales meeting. They were just going to throw it away, but I thought you maintenance guys would enjoy it."

He extended his hand and we shook. "My name is Wink and I'm the park human resources vice president."

"Hi I'm Dale." Sure enough, his name tag read Wink. What was it with employee names at this park, anyway?

"Wow one of the big dogs," Josh added, smiling stupidly. I flinched. He was a social buffoon.

"Yea," Wink continued, looking suspiciously at Josh. "Anyway, we had a couple of these wonderful deli and fruit trays made up by our spectacular food service department, and rather than chuck this one in the dumpster I thought you maintenance guys might like it.

It was a sad tray. Much of the fruit had been eaten. Several strawberry caps lay on one side. Most of the remaining grapes had brown spots. One cantaloupe slice had a bite taken from it. There were still dozens of slices of tired-looking bologna, ham and turkey rolled and speared with a toothpick, as well as several triangles of different cheeses. All of it had been pawed over.

Josh walked over, picked up several pieces of everything and started shoving it in. "This is great, free food, thanks," he uttered, his mouth brimming with turkey and Monterey jack cheese. He used his finger to scoop honey-mustard out of a plastic cup. For once his grin was eating meat and fruit with honey-mustard instead of shit.

"You're welcome young man," Wink acknowledged, smiling broadly. He obviously loved having his ass kissed. "How about you? Dale? You like deli meat and fruit? Help yourself, all you want."

I looked at it. Is it just me, I thought, or would anybody else be insulted by this? How did I know someone didn't lick everything on this platter? Or sneeze over it? Wink still stood there, looking at me, and I got the impression he wasn't leaving until I sampled his second-hand food that was otherwise destined for a landfill. He honest to God thought he was doing us a favor by bringing us trash.

"I'm really not much of a meat or a fruit eater," I lied.

"Go on."

"Seriously I'm not hungry."

Wink furrowed his brow. "But everybody likes fruit, especially if it's free, right? I know you maintenance guys love free stuff."

"It's just that ..."

"What?" Wink leaned in to me, his eyes narrowing.

I took a deep breath. What was I doing? It was my first day on the job. Was I begging to be fired?

"I just think it would have been nice to bring us a food tray that had not been picked over by another department."

Time itself stopped.

Josh froze in the middle of a bite of a strawberry.

Wink lowered his head and looked puzzled. "Excuse me?"

"Well, you said you were just going to throw this away." The words tumbled out automatically. "I mean no disrespect, but ..."

"But what?" Wink propped one foot up on the seat in front of me to make himself look more imposing. It was a power move.

But it made me stand my ground. "You brought in something for us that was going to get thrown away. This sends a clear message that maintenance doesn't deserve new fruit trays."

Wink seemed unperturbed on the outside. "And rather than throw it away I brought it in here for you guys – who I never regard as second class, by the way." His face got red and he became more animated. "I didn't have to bring it here, you know. I could have thrown it away."

Since he unwittingly was making my argument for me, I raised up and made eye contact. This was the confrontational behavior that got me in trouble in college with certain professors, a student council president and particularly a certain cop after a markedly raucous campus demonstration against Iran in 1978. "If you were going to throw it away, it's trash. I'm sorry, but I really ..."

"No, no, I understand," Wink announced far too loudly as he picked up the tray. I could see a few of the guys gathered outside the door, milling about, pretending not to notice my encounter with Wink. "I understand some people don't appreciate it when a company tries to make their rainy day a little more pleasant by bringing in a special treat that they certainly were not obligated to do." His face was redder and his voice got louder and faster. I suddenly felt like he was going to punch me or fire me but instead he picked up the food tray and turned to leave.

"If that's the way you guys feel I appreciate that and don't worry I won't insult you any more by bringing you free food. Hey, have a nice goddamn day, okay?"

He stormed out of the lunch room with the huge tray, wielding it over his shoulder like a pissed-off waiter in a failing white-top restaurant in Jerkwater, Alabama. A couple of the guys in the shop watched him leave then entered the break room. They were furious.

"Way to go, new guy," Bill angrily declared. "That's the end of the fucking free food."

"Damn if you haven't had one hell of a morning for your first day," Mudflap also asserted. "You and Thomas Edison there caused a million dollars' worth of damage on the white-water ride, now you cost us free food."

I tried to justify my position. "Don't you guys understand that he was bringing us trash? I mean he admitted it was going to a dumpster!"

Bill took a step toward me. He seemed to have the most to lose from my encounter with Wink. His enormous gut shimmied with rage. Hey, Bill, I wondered, what time was it?

"That man would bring in kitchen bags of fried chicken left over from group sales picnics and leave them in here," he hissed, bristling. "One time they had a hundred three-inch sub sandwich slices left from a company dinner. He brought them all for us. For free. I ate sub sandwich slices for a month. Great job asshole."

A casual observer would almost think the free food was more important than health insurance and a 401k. I sure thought so.

The guys left in a huff, leaving me alone in the break room with Josh in his high-water jeans and soaking wet Red Wing boots. Even Walter's sandwich looked mad at me.

Josh looked at his watch.

"Fifteen minutes." He bragged. "I just made another dollar doing nothing."

Chapter 8: in which I almost drown a boatload of guests

I WALKED WITH JOSH back into the shop after Wink left. I expected somebody to throw something at me for taking away the free food benefit, but the guys had all dispersed out into the park to monitor their rides while the park opened for the day. It was still cloudy and cold but at least it had stopped raining.

It dawned on me I had yet to see Walter, the guy who hired me.

Tex entered the shop after a few minutes of us standing around. He walked slowly, limping slightly after dumping the boom truck into the rapids reservoir.

"You okay, Tex?" I asked.

"I'll survive," he moaned as he unlocked the tool cage door and walked inside. "I know one damn thing I'll never back up that boom truck again." He closed and padlocked the door. He was back in prison after a disastrous parole.

I approached the window. "I heard you dumped the truck in the reservoir."

"Yep. It's sittin' right now ass end down in six feet of water. It looks like a bug trying to scramble up the slippery side of a swimming pool.

"What did Dink say?"

"You know, that asshole was more concerned about the truck than he was about me," Tex answered, with some distress. "After I backed off the wall down into the water he ran over and said this truck cost money."

Tex got more upset as he spoke, his voice breaking. "He never asked me … if I was hurt. And I was, my back is killing me. I hate this freaking job. I never drove anything bigger than a pickup truck in my life, and there I am backing this giant boom truck with no inspection and no goddamn mirrors on it down a goddamn pig path right over the edge of a fucking concrete wall and all the boss can say is don't hurt my truck. What kind of man does that?"

I was moved to see tears well up in Tex's eyes, and I suddenly felt a surge of sorrow for him. He had been profoundly affected by his accident and Dink's response to it.

I tried to be empathetic. "Yea, well the top management here seems a bit touchy about trucks and meat and cheese trays especially."

Nard the oral cancer turtle eater suddenly stepped to the tool cage window beside me.

"Tex, grab me a sledgehammer."

Tex cleared his eyes with a quick brush of his shirt sleeve. "I'll be damned if I'm giving you a sledge to kill that turtle."

Nard looked stunned. He had a wad of smokeless tobacco as big as his thumb in his lower lip. "I'm not gonna kill the turtle with it, I need it on the Gator coaster. I think a section of track is spreading open and it needs intermediate bolts put back that fell out."

Something seemed familiar about that situation.

Tex wouldn't budge. "I'm out of sledgehammers."

"The hell you are! I see two of them on the shelf back there." I looked, and Nard was right. Two brand new ones.

"They're reserved," Tex noted. "You can't have one."

"Are you Dale?" This was a new voice, from behind me.

I turned around at the new voice. It belonged to a slightly-built smaller guy with a weird grown-out 1950s DA haircut. He was in his late fifties, and his handshake was limp, almost nonexistent. His name tag read Wade.

"Yea I'm Dale," I admitted. "Are you mad at me for taking away the free fruit too?"

Nard rattled the locked door. "Come on Tex, I ain't got all day."

"Well, no," Wade continued over Tex's insistence, "Walter asked me to take you with me down to the Ghost River ride. We have a boat that needs work and I can't get it out by myself. Have you had your break?"

"Yea sure, I almost had some pawed-over fruit and a cup of toxic battery foam. But I'm supposed to see Judy for my orientation sometime this morning."

"Okay, then go on back and see her. That should take about thirty seconds. Then find me, so we can go down to the Ghost River."

Tex folded his arms, refusing to budge for Nard's request. "I am not going to be responsible for that turtle's death by sledgehammer."

I walked away from the tool cage window and through the office door beside the time clock. To my right was an open door, and inside was an attractive woman in her mid-30s. This was Judy.

I knocked on the open door and she looked up. "Well hello!" She welcomed me. "You must be Dale! Come on in."

I walked in, shook her hand and sat down when she offered me a chair. "So how has your first morning been?"

I wasn't sure how to answer, but the guys were correct, she was a remarkably beautiful woman. I was going to enjoy working around her. I decided, however, to be completely neutral in my answer to her question because my first morning had so far been a debacle. "It's been a learning experience."

She laughed, which was encouraging. "First days can be difficult, for sure, but orientation for maintenance is quite simple," she explained. "Don't do anything stupid, and ..."

"... don't pick up money," I finished.

She looked happily surprised. "Well yes! That will get you fired. And clock in on time."

She turned to some paperwork before she suddenly looked back at me, her expression more serious – almost sinister even. "Have you seen anyone picking up money?"

Gulp. I was about to provide her a non-threatening, non-implicating generic answer when she hit me with another one.

"Have you heard anyone say anything bad about Mr. Hutton?"

"... No, not at all," I stuttered, taken aback by her line of questioning. What was her angle anyway?

She suddenly smiled again. Her dual personalities kind of gave me the creeps. "I'll put you a timecard by the clock. Don't clock in more than five minutes before or after your shift. It was good meeting you, Dale! Good luck working here."

I got up and left, baffled by my meeting. I walked into the shop where Wade waited for me.

"Alrighty – consider yourself oriented." Wade clapped his hands and rubbed them together. "The ride just opened so we can get the operator to dispatch us the boat we need. We have a leaker that needs to come out. Probably just a stopped-up flipper."

"Nard," Wade declared as we turned to leave, "let that damn turtle go."

"No way," Nard insisted, turning to face Wade after unsuccessfully negotiating a sledgehammer from Tex. "That turtle's good eatin'."

Wade was dogged. "It'll take you hours to skin it, gut it and clean it, then it will have to stew overnight. In the end it will be tough, stringy and greasy. It ain't worth it. Let it go."

Wade seemed to have experience with turtles. And a sense of compassion. I kind of liked the guy for that.

But Nard wouldn't budge. "Naah, you're full of shit, that turtle's good eatin'."

I followed Wade across the truck parking area as Nard continued his negotiations with Tex over a sledgehammer. We got in his truck and he lit a Winston and drove us around a park perimeter road. We passed the rapids ride driveway, crossed the former railroad tracks from earlier and drove under the Gator coaster, which was preparing to open by cycling trains. I heard that scary *bangalangalangalang* sound again.

"You hear them pickup wheels?" Wade asked me.

"Is that what's making that noise?"

"Yea, the ride needs more pickup steel on the hills," he explained. My respect for him continued to grow. "The wheels are hitting bare wood in spots. Sounds almost too like the track is spreading open, like Nard said. I told Barnyard about it but of course he ignored me."

I thought about what Nard said at the tool cage window, and what Barnyard told me that morning. Maybe he was telling Tex the truth about why he needed a sledgehammer.

"You know a lot about coasters and cooking turtles," I told Wade.

"No, I don't know nothing about turtles, I made all that up," he confessed. "Nard's always killing then trying to cook and eat something. One day fishing last summer, he caught a mess of mud toads and claimed they were good eatin'. Damn near poisoned his family. His boy spent 2 days in the hospital."

We continued on through more woods before arriving at an electric gate. Wade keyed it open and then drove up to a large double door at the back of a wooden and concrete building. This was the back of the Ghost River ride in the rear of Frontier Village. I saw a security guard sweeping with a "litter-getter" on the other side of the security fence in preparation of the coming crowd.

"By the way, you've probably already heard this, but don't be fooled by Judy," he almost whispered to me. "She looks great and will charm the hell out of you – but she's a spy for Byram, the vice president."

Well, that explained a lot. "I'll keep that in mind."

"Have you ever ridden the Ghost River?" Wade asked as he got out and hoisted his toolbox out of the truck bed.

It was one of those rides that you rode once then never rode again. It was fun and all, and I guess young kids liked it. It was a slow boat ride in an enclosed building through several themed areas. There was lots of cheesy animated stuff going on, like skeletons hoisting beer steins at a banquet table, tombstones rocking back and forth, a fat lady laughing and what not.

"A few years ago," I answered. "I found it rather forgettable."

We entered through the huge doors into a dry-dock area with a motorized hoist and trolley on an overhead I-beam. A maintenance section of the water ride flowed through dry-dock. It was like a railroad side track but with water. That is where boats were taken off the ride when they needed work. Heavy black lightproof curtains hung at both ends where they entered through the wall on the right then exited on the far left.

Wade set down his red toolbox, rubbed his hands and lit a Winston. "Have you seen the TV room?"

"No."

Wade motioned for me to follow him. I could hear the booming music and sound effects from the ride. We turned right to a door tucked in a dark corner. Wade knocked twice, opened it, greeted a young male ride operator and we walked inside.

The room was about ten feet square and filthy dirty but toasty due to the heating unit in the wall. The operator – a kid named Floyd, according to his name tag – was sitting in a straight-back plastic chair in front of a bank of nine TV screens. Each screen projected a different part of the ride, which was monitored from beginning to end by infrared video cameras.

"The cameras were put in the ride for maintenance and monitoring purposes," Wade told me. "Since people were riding in the dark, they try to get away with stuff, not knowing they are on camera the entire time,"

"What kinds of things have you seen people do?" I asked Floyd.

"What don't they do," Floyd admitted with much defeat without taking his eyes off the monitors. "Last summer I pulled TV duty the whole month of July. Apparently, July is blowjob month on the Ghost River. About every tenth boat that drifts through I saw a guy sitting there with a smile on his face and his girlfriend's head in his lap."

My mouth dropped open as Floyd continued. "A few brave guests attempt sex in the dark. Twice last summer I saw somebody with their ass parked off the side of the boat, takin' a dump in the water. That's a code 99, and we have to shut the ride down. Women change their tampons and pads and drop them in the water. There's this college punk challenge where they pull pints of booze out when they enter the tunnel and try to drink it all before the ride is over. I've seen people try to switch boats. They can't see the cameras but I unfortunately see them. If people think they can get away with it they'll try anything. But they straighten up when I yell at them over the intercom."

"What do you say when you see them?"

"We have a script of responses, which is pretty good at scaring them back into their seats. Depends on the situation."

I watched the monitors as Floyd explained. I mostly saw a bunch of empty boats drifting through the ride in various scenes at differing angles in spooky, grey infrared broadcasts. Once in a while I saw a couple people in them. So far, they were behaving themselves.

"What do you say to people actually having sex?"

"I try to wait until the perfect right moment – then with the volume all the way up I say 'sit up straight in your boat please!' That usually kills their enthusiasm and jerks them to attention. It's actually pretty hilarious. We had a guy named Robert down here last year toward the end of the season. He got on the intercom and said 'stop boinking your girlfriend in your boat please.' Of course, he got fired for going off-script."

"Okey dokey Dale let's get that boat off," Wade interrupted, rubbing his hands together.

"See ya, Floyd."

"I'm not Floyd. This is somebody else's name tag. I forgot mine today. My name's Chip. They'll give me all-day bathroom duty if I get seen without a name tag. The only thing worse than TV duty is bathroom duty."

"Then see ya, Chip."

Wade and I left the lonely, dark and disturbed netherworld of the TV room and walked back to the dry dock area.

"I'll tell ya how this works," Wade instructed me, rubbing his hands to warm them. "I call the board operator." He pointed to a wall phone behind us. "The board operator will tell me the number of the boat we have to take off, and he'll tell me the number of the boat in front of it. We'll go out here through this little door into the ride."

He pointed at a low door to the right of dry-dock. "And we'll wait for the first boat to pass. After it goes by, we switch a little gate in the ride that will divert the leaking boat through these curtains into dry-dock. We then slide the gate back so no more boats come in here."

Wade walked me over to a control box that hung from a black cord from the overhead hoist. "We use this to lower the lift frame into the boat and pick it up out of the water to pull off the flipper and let it drain. The flipper keeps water from going in the boat but allows it to drain out on the lift. Usually a boat fills up because a piece of trash gets in the flipper. Then I call the operator and we open a gate on the exit side of dry-dock to put it back in service."

"Sounds like a plan." Inside the ride I could hear the sounds of pirates cat-calling and singing, ghosts wailing, a fat woman laughing and weird music playing throughout the ride's booming sound system. I wondered how anyone had sex or could produce a bowel movement in such an environment. Wade looked at his watch.

"It's 10:35, so the ride is officially open." Wade picked up the A-phone and pushed the main operator button. "Is this Janice? Janice, this is Wade back at dry-dock. Which boat is leaking? 18?"

"And which boat is right in front of 18. Uh huh. Okay. Do a late dispatch for us. Thanks."

Wade hung up the phone. "Come on with me." I followed him over to the far right of the heavy curtain to a door hidden in the wall of the ride. He opened the door and we walked inside the ride and were suddenly immersed in the middle of a pirate shipwreck. The music and sound effects boomed, skeletons in costume swayed back and forth, and red, blue and green strobes flashed and flickered. I suddenly felt like a little kid again, staring in wonder at the hokey electric and air-powered animation and sound effects. It was almost exciting. How weird to be buried in the guts of the excitement earning money and not merely watching.

"Now when we see boat number 23 go by, we open that gate." Wade shouted over the noise, pointing down in the water to a little diversion gate hooked in the closed position to the concrete wall. "Just unloop the chain then shove it with your foot. The water will help push it open. I'll tell you when."

Boat 29 drifted by with two teenagers kissing in the rear seat. They couldn't see us at all. Floyd was right; this was a popular make out ride. Chip, I mean. Whatever. A minute later boat 23 floated by with a young family, gazing intently at the animation. A little girl sat huddled close to her mother, staring at the scenery, either scared or simply freezing to death. You could see your breath inside this pneumonia hole.

Once number 23 was past, Wade told me to unlatch the little diverter gate and shove it open, which I did. It drifted easily in the slow-moving water. After a minute boat 18 drifted slowly around the corner toward us. It was empty of guests but filled up to the seats with water. Wade and I shoved it through the curtain into the maintenance area. The system worked like a charm. Wade and I walked out the little door to lift it out.

I grabbed the hoist control while Wade pushed an A-frame over the boat when it stopped against a 6x6 wooden block. "Lower 'er down," he ordered.

I pushed the down button and lowered the steel lifting frame over the boat. Wade snapped four hooks over eye-bolts on the boat. "Now lift 'er up. Slow, she's going to be heavy."

I pressed the up button and the hooks snapped taut and the boat slowly groaned out of the water, the hoist chain creaking under the weight of the hundreds of gallons of water. Once it was up a couple of feet Wade signaled me to stop. He reached around behind the boat's bottom somewhere and popped off the rubber flipper. Sure enough it was stopped up. It had what looked like a wadded pair of women's underwear stuck in it. Water gushed from the drain hole like a fire hose.

"That's what I thought," Wade tossed the panties into a nearby trash can when suddenly another boat appeared into the maintenance area – this one full of guests, beating through that curtain.

"The gate!" Wade yelled at me, "didn't you close the gate?"

Shit. No, I forgot all about closing that diverter gate. Now another boat – this one full of six adult guests – was drifting into dry-dock.

"Sir? I don't think we're supposed to be going this way," a woman in the front seat suggested to me as Wade panicked and ran through the little door to close that gate so no more boats would come through.

No, you're not, I would have said if I didn't suddenly realize this boat full of people was going to run into the boat I had dangling in the air and draining hundreds of gallons of water – right at head level. This was about to turn into an accident that would surely get me fired.

I dropped the hoist button and tried to stop the boat full of people only it was too heavy. Where the hell was Wade? Why wasn't he back yet?

"We're going to hit that boat!" a man yelled, seeing that the ass end of the boat was at their neck level. They were going to have to lie all the way down to avoid whacking their heads on the pissing beast dangling ahead of them.

Thinking fast I grabbed the hoist button again. Pressing the up button, I raised the draining boat up another foot until the hoist chain bottomed out. The mechanism groaned and swayed with the weight of the water-filled boat, still gushing gallons of water from the rear drain hole like an opened hydrant on a hot New York City sidewalk.

The people were about to get drowned by the draining water. Or crushed, if the hoist was unable to hold such a heavy boat in the air that long.

Sure enough, each row of the three-seated boat passed directly under the gushing drain, drenching the six guests. The ones not getting drenched looked up at the bottom of the boat not six inches over their heads. They were all pissed and hollering and cussing at me, facing the dual threats of getting squashed or drowned or both.

"That boat's gonna fall on us!"

"Get us away from that leaking boat!"

"Hey jerk! Get us outta here!"

Where in the bloody hell was Wade?

The boat suddenly stopped against the 6x6 block that I neglected to lift up. If I had, they would have floated safely out from under the leaker and back onto the ride. Now there were stopped under the gushing boat, unable to move, locked in by seat belts like an electric chair.

I froze.

But I had options. I could drop everything, take a leisurely stroll through the park, get back to the shop, punch out and walk to my car. I could drive home, take a nap, then buy a newspaper and begin again the process of circling classified ads, looking for another job. I could have done a whole lot of things but I did the one thing I knew was the right at that moment.

I panicked.

My panic attack began when I tried to shove the boat full of people backwards out from under the leaking boat. The current was too strong, however, and the boat was too heavy. Water was beating on a woman's face like a waterfall.

Suddenly Wade appeared. He was soaking wet from the waist down because he had to jump in the ride to stop another boat full of people from diverting out of the ride while he closed the gate. The boat had run over his foot and his cigarettes and pocket protector had fallen out, washing away all his pocket-sized tools.

"Good Lord Dale what are you doing!"

An excellent question, Wade. What was I doing? Five months ago, I was a college senior, flying high with a 2.7 GPA, a meal card and an unpaid but rewarding production job with the university literary magazine. I was at the top of my game, respected as a student art director and the life of the party. I planned protests against university administration and against unfair police tactics. I wrote op-eds for the student newspaper about these perceived atrocities against student rights. Then I graduated during the worst recession in American history, and I sent out fifty inquiry letters and this was the only paying job I could find. This is what post-college life had to offer me. And I was doing it badly.

Wade acted fast and raised the wooden stopper block. The boat full of people – with water nearly up to the seats – drifted slowly out of dry-dock, the guests now threatening me with my job and a good ass-kicking at the exit of the ride if only I would meet them there. I declined.

It was a simple solution that I didn't think of.

The people beat their way angrily through the curtain at the other end of the maintenance area then re-entered the ride, soaking wet but out of sight and now out of mind.

Without a word, Wade put the flipper back on the boat in the air once it stopped leaking. He lowered it back down in the water then shoved it forward, putting it back in service. The empty boat floated through the curtain and disappeared into the darkness, the yo-ho-hoing of the mechanical pirates and the other light and noise effects of the ride.

I suspected he was also in the midst of a panic attack. "I think it's best if I took you back to the shop."

Suddenly I heard Chip over the loudspeaker. "Please sit up straight in your boat please." I wondered what he had seen.

We walked in silence back out to the truck, got in and he drove me back up to the big door without a word. When I got out, he gunned the truck and drove off. I walked back inside like I had been beaten with sticks.

Tex stuck his head around the tool cage door at me. "Lunch is from twelve to one young man. Better get washed up."

The time clock thunked 11:57. I had quite a morning.

Chapter 9: in which I go to lunch, learn about crackers and meet the craft-tech tool guy from hell

NOT WANTING TO BE THE FIRST ONE in the break room for lunch my first day on the job, I hung around, trying to look like I was doing something. Judy walked into the roll-up door. I was about to wave at her when she shot me a hateful look and disappeared into another door that went down a hall to her office.

Well that was weird.

Barnyard suddenly appeared through the big door. "Holy moly there Andy."

"Holy moly," Tex answered. But the life was gone from his voice.

"Don't go drivin' no more boom trucks there Andy."

"I am finished driving boom trucks, Kingfish."

"Lunch time ain't it," Barnyard announced to me as he walked past toward the break room door. *Snock*.

Sure. I dutifully followed him in.

I bought a package of cheese crackers at a 7-Eleven on my way to work that morning and that was all I had. I assumed the employee cafeteria would be open but it was closed because of a gas problem. I sat down at one of the tables and started unwrapping my crackers. Walter's bacteria-laden sandwich whispered but I passed.

As I sat there, Bill came in, his shirt again soaking wet. "Rooty patootie," he announced. "I hope you haven't screwed up anymore since you had our free food taken away."

"No," I responded. "Everything's been great. My performance has been superb."

As Bill walked around behind the locker wall to change into a dry shirt, Mudflap walked in, holding a brown bag. "What say, Spider-rider." He sat at the middle of the three tables.

Wade came in, also holding a brown bag lunch. He looked at me and shook his head, either in sympathy or disgust, I couldn't tell. "Those people in that boat reported you to guest services," he told me. "Dink hauled my ass on the carpet and said I needed to hold your hand the rest of the day. I told him it was an honest rookie mistake. They gave those people free passes but they stayed blowed up."

"What are you talking about Wade?" Mudflap asked. "What people. What passes? Blowed up about what? What did newbie do this time?"

"Nothing." Wade set his lunch bag down at the end table beside Barnyard before he walked into the bathroom. I appreciated his discretion.

Josh entered the break area in his high-water boot-cut jeans, grinning stupidly, his white socks flashing over his Red Wing boots as he walked. He sat down across from Mudflap.

"If you'd been wearing those high-water pants at the rapids ride you wouldn't have gotten wet when the pumps came on," Mudflap informed him.

Josh just kept grinning, unable to formulate a witty response at such short notice.

"Earth to Josh. You ain't been snooping again have ya?" Mudflap continued.

"Nope."

"Where you been anyway?"

"Had to take an inspection sheet to the Phantom Tower."

"For who?"

Josh hesitated. "Operations couldn't find it." I could tell he was lying. He did it as badly as Barnyard.

The Phantom Tower was a 200-ft tall steel observation tower built into the Steel Phantom lift hill. People took an elevator to the top, and it offered unobstructed views of the surrounding countryside. And for a quarter, guests could look through these powerful free-standing binoculars at the tree-stump covered countryside.

Bill walked out of the locker area wearing a dry red-and-white checkerboard shirt, pinning on his nametag. Mudflap started laughing. "Damn 10-till-2, you look like a table for six at Pizza Hut."

"Screw you." He sat down across from me and took an identical package of cheese crackers out of his lunch bag. He looked at mine.

"Where'd you get those crackers?" he asked.

"7-Eleven."

"What'd you pay for them?"

I shrugged. "I don't know. Sixty-five cents maybe."

"Good God all mighty! You see these crackers?" He held up his own after tearing them open.

"Yea ...?"

"I got them at Price Club. Exact same crackers. They came in a box of 250 packs. In bulk I paid seventeen and one-half cents a pack. You paid sixty-five cents. You got ripped off." Bill beamed arrogantly as he popped one in his mouth. He obviously knew the fine points of cracker purchasing.

"New guy must be made of money!" Mudflap laughed.

Now I didn't even want to eat my goddamn crackers.

"Hey Bill," Mudflap asked, "why did Josh have to take another inspection sheet up into the tower anyway? Did they lose it?"

"Damn if I know," Bill responded before he looked at Josh. "You take the stairs to the top?"

Josh shook his head no, then yes. His face was red. He was suffering inside. Some secret was killing him.

"I remember stringing the Christmas lights on top of that damn tower in 1974," Barnyard chimed in. "I was so scared I was crying. Pucker factor 9.8 out of 10."

Mudflap laughed. "I hear ya. I had to change the top red aircraft beacon light a few years ago. If there had been a glue stick between my cheeks I would have pinched it clean in two."

Wade came out of the bathroom and sat down with his lunch beside Barnyard, who had started a game of solitaire. He took out a piece of veal apparently left over from his dinner last night. He looked sadly at it before he looked out the lunch room door, which was blocked open.

"Hey Bill?"

"Yea?"

"The Craft-Tech tool guy's out in the shop."

"Dammit!" Bill dropped his cheap Price Club crackers, struggled to his feet and trotted quickly into the bathroom, disappearing just as a stern grey-haired man in a yellow and black Craft-Tech tool uniform and smoking a pipe walked slowly into the break room carrying a clipboard. A black cloud descended as he scrutinized the gathered crowd. He was an independent contractor who sold Craft-Tech-brand tools and safety equipment on-site out of a truck. He looked a lot like Christopher Lee.

"How you boys doin'." His voice was flat and moldy.

"Broke," Barnyard muttered. "No money for tools."

Mudflap took a big bite of sandwich. "Hey Lurch, you come here to ruin our toilets again?"

The Craft-Tech guy turned to him. "I don't know what you're talking about."

"The hell you don't. That thing you left in the toilet last Friday. Walter had to beat it up with a coat hanger."

Why do I have to keep hearing this story?

The Craft-Tech guy was unfazed, then he took the pipe out of his mouth. He had the personality of an unpaid undertaker. "Anybody seen Bill?"

"Haven't seen him," Barnyard retorted without looking from his solitaire game. "No wait, he's hiding from you in the toilet stall."

No honor among thieves.

The Craft-Tech guy glanced at Bill's hastily abandoned lunch then walked to the bathroom. He opened the door and stood with it open.

"Bill, I know you're in here."

Bill remained quiet. Craft-Tech guy looked down at the floor.

"I can see your 10-till-2 feet."

Quiet.

"Hey Lurch, close the damn bathroom door!" Barnyard ordered. "We got people eating food here."

The Craft-Tech guy was unfazed. "You can't keep hiding from me, Bill."

Quiet.

"I need that check."

Quiet.

"I'm sure you want to keep working on the Bump'em cars."

Still quiet. I thought that was an interesting thing to say. Why would the Craft-Tech guy threaten someone with working on Bump'em cars?

The Craft-Tech guy finally let the bathroom door close. He walked back to the center of the lunch room and stopped. He glared at me and Josh before he removed his pipe and pointed it at me.

"You fellas are new. You need quality tools."

"Josh needs an anti-dumbass device," Mudflap interrupted. "You got any of those in your truckload of high-dollar shit?"

"Craft-Tech tools are the best tools in the world," the guy answered forcefully. "They have a lifetime guarantee. Once you buy one Craft-Tech tool you will never buy another one."

I wondered if Craft-Tech guy realized what he just implied with that last line. He badly needed to refine his sales patter.

"Dale there can afford to buy everything on your truck," Mudflap continued. "He's made of money. He buys crackers at 7-Eleven instead of Price Club."

And Mudflap needed to shut up.

Josh looked up stupidly. "Me! I need quality tools!"

"Atta boy," Craft-Tech guy replied to Josh. "Meet me at the truck after lunch and I will set you up."

"I buy all my tools off the Buffalo Forge truck," Barnyard interjected, looking up from his sandwich and his game.

"Buffalo tools are shit," the Craft-Tech guy coughed up, more as a threat than a comment. "Made out of plastic and pot metal."

"Holy moly there Andy!" Barnyard answered. His universal response for everything. But it was true, his tools were crap.

Wade jumped into the conversation. "Somebody want a piece of veal?"

Lump walked into the break room carrying a black lunch bucket and one of those old-time giant green Eisenhower-era Stanley thermos bottles.

"My titties stay black and blue all the time," Barnyard laughed.

Lump didn't seem to be amused. "You grab my titties one more time I'll string your ass up on that chain hoist."

"Holy moly!"

"Lump you want a piece of veal?"

"No, I'm good Wade. I got leftover homemade spaghetti."

Snock.

Lump sat down, opened his lunch bucket and took out a huge Tupperware bowl of spaghetti. It looked less homemade and more Boyardee.

The Craft-Tech guy furrowed his brow, put his pipe in his mouth and sucked all the air from the room. He hooked Josh but he was low-hanging fruit.

"Bill can't stay in that toilet all day," he muttered while he flicked a Zippo lighter into that stinking pipe.

"Somebody please eat this veal."

The rail-thin guy with Chunky on his name tag came in the room. He sat down across from me and lit a cigarette, glaring at me through his thick, smeared glasses. Uh oh.

"May I help you," I innocently asked.

"We were supposed to get a vegetable tray with chips and dips over in the auto shop left over from a corporate lunch in the Tally-Ho room," he grunted. I suddenly knew where this was going. "It never showed up. I called food service and they told me why."

"Dale got our free food taken away," Barnyard announced without looking away from his cards. "But he's made of money – maybe he can buy us all lunch."

"Yea, what they told me," Chunky echoed. "The memo from HR said from now on all leftover food was going to get thrown away."

I shrugged. "Sorry about that. But maybe Wink can retrieve it from the dumpster and still bring it over."

"Sorry, hell, I got no lunch," Chunky grimaced before he got up and stormed out.

"Anybody seen Walter?" Wade suddenly asked, thankfully changing the subject.

"It's not my day to watch him," Barnyard answered, still turning over cards. *Snock.*

"I think he's still at the Scrambler. That actor almost got killed last night. Dink is gonna make him stand down there with that county inspector all day if he needs to or not."

A man I never saw before walked into the break room, carrying four heavy cartons in his arms. His name tag read Merv. His work uniform was clean and starched, and his hair was dyed and unusually wavy, like a 1940s movie star. He was one of the ride mechanic supervisors, like Walter, the mystery supervisor who hired me for some reason and whom I had yet to see in person today.

Barnyard looked up at him from losing at solitaire. "Whatcha got there Merv the perv?"

Merv sat the cartons proudly on the vacant middle table across from Mudflap. They were unopened cartons of cole slaw and potato salad. "Free slaw and salad," he announced, popping open the cartons. "That's what it is."

Sing hosannas. The free food benefit had been restored.

All the guys quickly dug into the free slaw and potato salad. Not me – it wouldn't have been right for me, seeing as how I screwed everything up earlier with Wink, even though I was starving. Somebody laid some paper bowls and KFC sporks beside the cartoons. The buffet was open, and the guys loaded up.

Wade was the last one to serve himself. He looked at the cartons. "What dumpster did these come out of?"

"They didn't come out of no dumpster," Merv explained. "It's good food."

Wade spooned some out on his plate. He noted it looked fresh and smelled okay. "Did Wink give these to you?"

"No, I got them down at the Tennessee Kitchen. They were giving them away."

The Craft-Tech guy looked at his watch, sat down at the end of my table and stared at me. He smelled like pipe smoke and Dippity-Doo hair gel. "If you're going to work here you better get some high-quality tools, like your buddy here," he warned in that undercooked Frankenstein voice. He was more than a black cloud over the break room, he was a plague – a St. Vitus Dance.

"I know but it's my first day and I don't have any money."

Barnyard snorted. "You spent it all buying crackers at 7-Eleven." *Snock*.

"Your money's no good to me," Craft-Tech guy insisted. "We have deferred payment options, payroll deduction. We can make it work. You can't do this job without tools."

"The way my morning is going I'll get fired before I'll even need them."

"Hah!" Mudflap laughed between creamy mouthfuls of free potato salad, "Newbie got that right!"

"You'll get fired anyway if your supervisor realizes you're working with no tools."

"You know what," I suggested, my blood pressure rising, "now you're just starting to piss me off."

Craft-Tech guy's eyebrows raised. "Oh, so the nobody seasonal worker is getting pis …"

"Boys," Merv interrupted, trying to stop our discussion from escalating. "Want some slaw? Potato salad? All you want."

The Craft-Tech guy was not backing down. "All I'm saying is that to properly do this job you need the proper tools – and I'm not talking about that Buffalo junk neither. Those thin-walled sockets will shatter on you. I'd hate to see you pulling 140 foot-pounds of torque on a bolt on the coaster track and have the socket shatter. You might as well put a gun in your mouth like that guy Bob and blast your brains all over that wall than buy that cheap junk."

Bob the guy with the snake on his face was legendary around there.

Craft-Tech guy continued, just a touch friendlier than before. "Now take Bill, who's hiding from me in the toilet stall? He bought our top of the line deluxe master mechanic's set. Over 2,000 of the highest quality pieces in a state-of-the-art roll-around steel cabinet. Everything he will ever need, and all with a lifetime guarantee."

"Where's Nard?" somebody asked. "He out there eating that damn turtle?"

"Guess I'll just throw away this veal if nobody wants it."

"Holy moly there Andy!"

"You need steel-toe shoes too," the Craft-Tech guy went on as he again lit his pipe and chugged out noxious clouds of Captain Creosote, his droning monotone making me just as nauseous. "We have a wide selection out on the truck. Come on out and take a look. No charge just to look. Unless you're planning to cut your feet off."

"My shoes will rot before I'll buy those pricey Craft-Tech shoes," Barnyard declared, helping himself to another heaping bowl of Merv's free Tennessee Kitchen cole slaw. He was serious – his shoes were completely rotten already. Duct tape was the only thing holding them together. "I saw one pair on your truck that cost $145. My health insurance don't cost $145."

The Craft-Tech guy sucked on his pipe, removed it and blew twin contrails through his nostrils. He showed no emotion as he sluggishly turned to Barnyard, like an animated skeleton in the Ghost River ride that was on fire.

"One day, somebody's going to take those shoes off you, beat you with them and burn them. Might just be me. And you'll need that health insurance so you better hang on to it."

Barnyard was unfazed by Craft-Tech guy's overt threat. "Holy moly there, Lurch!"

"Gracious!" Merv blurted. "Such worldly talk."

You know, all I wanted was to get some quiet time and eat my stupid crackers after my hellish morning but the Craft-Tech guy was slowly killing me with his disgusting pipe and insipid and intimidating sales rap. I was about to get up and leave just as Merv the free slaw guy took a radio call.

"Base to 4-2, *scratch*."

Merv wrestled his radio from the holster. "4-2 go ahead."

The Craft-Tech guy rose like Nosferatu in his coffin, walked to the bathroom and opened the door again. "I'll be back Friday, Bill. I need that check for $752 or I garnish your wages for the entire balance at 35 percent interest. Pay me now or pay me later."

"Be advised the Steel Phantom will be opening today and needs the inspection sheet signed. *Scratch*."

Craft-Tech guy let the bathroom door close. He was a hard case. Craft-Tech Mafia.

On his way out he grabbed Bill's sandwich and crackers, shoved them in the bag, then pointed to Josh. "My truck in fifteen." He dropped Bill's lunch on the floor, crushed it flat with his heel, then chucked it in the trash can. He then left without saying goodbye to anybody.

"Good grief, they want to open the Phantom after all," Merv moaned after holstering his radio. "Guest services got a lot of complaints about rides being closed. Dink wants as many open as possible. Guess I'll go down there and sign the sheet." He suddenly looked at me and introduced himself.

"I'm Merv, by the way."

"Hi Merv, I'm Dale."

"Are you in college?"

"I graduated."

"Our colleges have been infiltrated by communists."

"I'm not surprised, I knew a communist in college," I explained. "His name was Cliff." This was true – Cliff the commie we called him. He was a numb-nuts with a 1.6 GPA. Halfway through his junior year he flunked out and went back to live with his parents. Fuck capitalism, but I need $5, daddy.

"You know I have a scripture and prayer service back in the paint shop Monday through Friday before work," Merv noted. "It would do you good to come. It will get that communist secular dogma out of your system and introduce you to the sword of the Lord."

Bill came out of hiding from the toilet stall when the coast was clear. He sat down and stared sadly where his lunch used to be, which included his sensibly-priced Price Club crackers. "Dammit."

"What, is that like the third or fourth time?" Mudflap asked him.

"When I was a kid, I seen this preacher at a revival in Norfolk," Merv continued, refusing to leave me alone. "I'll never forget him – he had a second head growing out the middle of his back. But that head didn't preach – his main head done all the preaching."

What?

"He had a great message of soul-winning and redemption out of his main head," Merv continued, as serious as this lunch break was painful. "That second head just hung there. Which head will you think with, the preacher asked? The one that just hangs there, smiling and blinking and going along, or the one that rejects worldliness and embraces the Lord? Think about it."

Oh, I'm thinking about it, all right.

I watched Merv leave the lunch room. "Did Merv really get that slaw and potato salad out of a dumpster," I asked Mudflap after shaking away the two-headed preacher story.

"I seriously doubt it," Mudflap responded. "Merv has a knack for finding decent food, not garbage. Bill, remember that time that guy delivering strawberries flipped his Cushman under the Gator? Merv drove up on the accident right after it happened."

"Yea," Bill recalled as he spooned out a giant bowl of potato salad. "the driver wasn't hurt but he was pinned. Merv picked up a gallon bucket of strawberries for himself before he helped the driver out from under the Cushman. Took them home to his family."

"The driver of that Cushman got half-shitty with him."

"Guess I can't blame him. Leave a man pinned while you pick up all his strawberries."

Dink suddenly burst into the break room. Nothing about him was subtle. He looked at me and pointed, his finger three inches from my face. "You need to fill in an accident report with loss prevention."

I was confused. "For what?"

"For when you fell in the rapids ride."

"That was Josh." I pointed at him across from me. Dink's finger swung over at Josh instead.

"You need to fill in an accident report with loss prevention."

Josh nodded. "Okay."

"Also, after you do that you're fired."

Josh's face dropped, his shit-eating grin falling from his lips smeared creamy white with free cole slaw. "What?"

"Stand up."

Josh submissively stood.

"Empty your pockets," Dink ordered.

Everybody hushed. Josh grinned nervously. "Um ..."

"You heard me."

Josh put his hands in his pockets and pulled out about $20 in quarters. They weren't dirty like the ones from the flume ride, they were clean and shiny. He dropped them in a pile on the table right in front of me. A small silver key was mixed in with them.

Dink looked at him. "How did you get a key to the observation tower binoculars?"

"I found it," Josh stuttered, talking to the table.

"Where?"

"Um."

"You were seen by the Phantom operators opening the tower binoculars and taking the money," Dink explained. "Go see Harley down the hall in security. He'll take your statement on falling in the rapids then he'll take you to the gate. He agreed the park will not press charges as long as all the money and the key is returned."

Josh was going to take that long drive home talking to himself over $20, the same amount he would have made just by looking stupid for five hours – which came naturally to him. After Dink left, Josh could only stand there and look at the pile of quarters that just got him fired.

Dink suddenly burst in again. "Remember guys quarterly employee meeting in the conference room right after lunch. Except you Josh, you report to security."

Everybody except Bill started wadding their empty lunch bags and sweeping their spot at the tables, moaning about the quarterly meeting. Fired for eighty quarters, somebody commented.

"Told you not to pick up money you dumbass," Mudflap rebuked Josh as he walked past.

"Aren't you going to eat those high-dollar crackers?" Bill asked me, motioning to the uneaten pack in front of me.

"They're yours if you want them." Of course, he scooped them up.

Everybody left the lunch room, leaving Josh standing and staring at the pile of quarters.

"Sorry, Buddy," I whispered as I walked out. I would never see him again.

The time clock thunked 1:00.

Chapter 10: in which I attend my first quarterly meeting, meet Byram and learn of the park's experience with animals

AFTER LUNCH, EVERYBODY in the shop filed down a hallway beside the lunch room past some nondescript offices. In the first I saw Judy typing with one finger, but oddly there did not seem to be any paper in her typewriter carriage. In another I saw a barrel-shaped guy on hold on the phone. He had a Grainger tool catalog open on his desk. In another I saw I saw a redneck woman with impeccable bouffant hair leaned back behind an empty desk enjoying a cigarette. She stared back at me without smiling. She must have known I cost her the free food benefit.

I followed the guys into a conference room with a large table in the center, surrounded by over twenty-five plastic chairs. The room was an all-purpose training and meeting room. On the left side was a kitchenette area, with cabinets, a counter, sink and coffeemaker. A dry-erase board stood nearby, with the words "Park guests leave their common sense in their car trunks" written badly in dried green. On the other side was a medical training setup, complete with a "resusci-Annie" CPR training dummy, a stethoscope, blood pressure cuff, rolls of ace bandages and other medical paraphernalia.

The ride maintenance guys were joined by several guys from the carpenter shop, paint shop, fiberglass and millwright shops. Chunky from the auto shop strolled in, still scowling over the undelivered veggie tray.

The guys joked with each other as we waited for Dink, this Byram guy and some other managers to come in. One of the painters acted like he was receiving oral sex from resusci-Annie. Several guys laughed and cheered him on.

I imagined Floyd or Chip in the Ghost River TV room announcing "please stop having sex with resusci-Annie."

Nard the snapping turtle-eater came in furious about something and sat by himself.

"You full of delicious turtle, Nard?" one of the millwrights asked him.

"I catch who let my turtle go I'll beat them with that sledgehammer Tex won't give me," he fumed.

I watched Lump pick up a nearby stethoscope and I noticed the rubber tips on the earpieces were gone. He put the bare metal ends in his ears anyway and snuck in behind Barnyard, who was already seated at the table talking. He was in a playful mood. But I thought this wasn't going to end well.

"Just as well Nard, that turtle would have been worthless as a meal," someone commented.

Nard was unapologetic. "That turtle would have been good eatin'."

Then, just as Lump reached around Barnyard and placed the stethoscope diaphragm on his chest, Barnyard startled, grabbed the stethoscope, and gave it a hard yank.

Lump shrieked in agony as the bare metal tips ripped from his ears. He clapped both hands over his ears just as Dink, that Byram guy and a powerful black man in a police uniform leading Josh by the arm arrived in the room. They were just in time to watch Lump's floor show.

"Lump what the hell were you doing!" Barnyard shouted, "I didn't know what that was!" Lump, Dink and Byram could only stand, watch and wonder as Lump danced around the room, holding his ears and wailing.

"Better get him to first aid," somebody suggested. "He might have punctured eardrums." Lump jogged out on his own after Dink turned and pointed him toward the first aid building.

"Well, so much for the safety award," this Byram guy muttered as he called the meeting to order. Byram was Dink's boss, and he was the vice president of planning and development. He was in his late 50s, with skinny white arms and a pot belly that stretched his short sleeve plaid dress shirt to the breaking point, the bottom buttons screaming that they could not hold on much longer. I heard Byram had been at the park since it was a tobacco field.

Everyone finally settled down and paid attention.

"Welcome to everyone, especially you new folks, my name is Byram Hutton." He looked like he had dip in his lower lip. "You can look at the park employee organizational chart here on the wall and see that I am the one close to the top." I looked at the chart in a frame to Byram's left. He was third down from the top. The only ones above him were the General Manager and the asshole VP of human resources who brought us trash on a silver platter. Dink and some other managers were directly below him.

"It goes without saying that our 1980 season is not off to a very good start," he announced. "Even you maintenance guys can see that. Commercial shooting this past week was a disaster. The weather is hurting attendance. The rides aren't doing so well today either. A lot of weather downtime, and a lot of mechanical downtime."

Dink's face flared red. He did not care for public pronouncements of downtime under his watch.

"A few changes we're making right away before we open full time in two weeks," Byram continued. "First off we're getting rid of the monkeys down in Nipperville, our children's area. For those of you not familiar, we set a huge glass terrarium down there and put in about twenty of these cute little monkeys for the kids and parents to enjoy, with sticks and ropes and climbing things for whatever little monkeys do all day."

Some of the guys looked sideways at one another. Some were already stifling laughter.

"Turns out instead of climbing and playing, we paid six thousand dollars for cute little monkeys that masturbate all day. We've had more complaints than we have people in the park right now. So, the monkeys are going back tomorrow. I told the area operations supervisor to put a tarp over the cage before somebody calls child protective services."

"Or happy Harry," somebody mumbled.

The guys all suppressed laughter, as Byram made this mortifying announcement without cracking a smile. Apparently too, the happy Harry joke was an inside one I was not privy to.

"You guys think this is funny?" Byram demanded, getting irritated. "It's not funny it's sick – their little hands are a blur."

Byram was making things worse. Some guys covered their faces. I could see heads down and shoulders bouncing.

"It's not funny," Byram continued, jabbing a finger in the air and getting angrier. He just wouldn't shut up. "Some of you guys who think this is funny ought to deal with these parents. I'm dead serious you better stop laughing."

As the snickering finally subsided, Byram then turned the meeting over to the muscular policeman who still held Josh by the arm.

"Hey everybody I'm Harley Race, director of security. I asked Byram to move me up on the agenda since I have to escort a fired employee out the gate for stealing." Josh smiled sheepishly but still stupidly as he hung there by the upper arm like he was dangling from a chain hoist. Harley had him on display by a death grip.

"This young man here is a reminder that we don't snoop for money under rides. You will be fired, no questions asked. Just ask this young man." He shook Josh like he was a puppy that just peed on an expensive rug. In fact, Josh looked like a puppy that just peed on an expensive rug.

"He's now going out to his car. He's done. That's all I have. Thanks, Byram."

I could hear Josh telling Harley that he didn't have a car and he had to call his mom to come get him as Harley led him out by the arm. Byram stood back up.

"I don't have any news on the actor injured on the Scrambler last night so don't even ask me," he announced.

"Oh, and another thing," he added as an afterthought. "Barnyard? Tex? And the rest of you, we had a complaint of racial insensitivity about your Amos and Andy routines from a couple of colored people who overheard you. You need to stop that holy moly there Andy stuff."

Barnyard wasn't even listening, but Tex lowered his head in shame. I winced. *Colored people?* This is the eighties, for gosh sakes.

"Attendance projections for the 1980 season have been adjusted down again for the fifth time since last month," Byram read from a report. "As of today, we are expecting a total of four hundred fifteen thousand guests this season. That is an 18 percent decrease from last season, and a more or less 60 percent decrease from our top year of one million two hundred ten thousand in 1971."

He cleared this throat and kept reading silently, like the sad numbers were just sinking in.

"On a positive note I am proud to announce next year's 1981 project, pending results of our test marketing. It is a themed area called 'Hootin' Holler.' It will be a re-creation of a ramshackle West Virginia hillbilly mountain town, with shacks, a general store, a Baptist Church and cars up on blocks. We'll have live actors playing hillbillies laying around, drinking moonshine, chasing girls and what not. We'll stage shotgun weddings, bank robberies, shoot-outs and have lots of barefoot square dancing with guests pulled from the crowd. We'll move and re-theme two of our flat rides and probably add one more at a later date."

I was frankly, stunned. And the more Byram described this place the more horrified I became. "We'll convert Frontierville Pizza into an authentic mountain town diner, serving real food but labeled on the menu chitlins', possum and hog jowls, crap like that. There'll be a big

Coca-Cola drink stand shaped like a whiskey still dispensing cold drinks in plastic bottles with xxx on the label. It'll be located in that empty spot near Ford Lake, behind the Steel Phantom. This is continuing our five-year long-range initiative to alternate thrill rides with family attractions, and we expect this attraction to increase attendance by at least 25 percent, or at least get us back to 1976 levels."

Christ almighty. I had a girlfriend in college who spent her summers working in the Southwest Virginia coalfields as a med tech. She described nightmare scenarios of horrible living and working conditions, unemployment, high infant mortality, alcoholism, drug abuse, racial and class disparities and domestic violence that made me sick to my stomach. And now a theme park was going to create a family attraction out of that misfortune? I was appalled, I was …

… Outspoken. "That's awful."

It just kind of came out. Suddenly and without thinking, and right at a moment of total complete silence, I spoke my mind way louder than I ever intended.

The room froze. Everybody turned to me. Dink shot a look and his face flared again, like an angry iguana. Byram's mouth hung open before he confronted me.

"I beg your pardon?"

Oh crap. Here I go again. First, I pissed off the HR vice president, now I was about to piss off my boss's boss's boss.

"You have something to say," Byram directed again.

I cleared my throat. No going back now. "I said, that's awful. Sir."

Byram crossed his arms. Another power move – the top brass here were full of these moves. "Care to explain?"

"Well ..." My heart pounded and I could feel my face turning red. The entire room stared at me, holding its breath. Apparently, it was against ride maintenance protocol to doubt the words and deeds of the mighty Byram Hutton. I guess that's why he had his administrator Judy to look out for him. I must be the biggest blabbermouth idiot to ever work there.

"I just think Hootin' Holler is in bad taste."

"Bad taste." Byram smirked. I had put him on the spot, and he wasn't liking it. Some of the guys started to squirm.

The protest poured out of me. "You're taking the worst socio-economic aspects of a poor Appalachian town – unemployment, alcoholism, poverty, even unfair stereotypes like laziness, pedophilia and sexual assault – and twisting it into a fun-filled amusement park themed area. You're going show kids it's fun to drink bottles of moonshine straight out of a still. You're going charge guests $29 to experience the horror people in any hollow of Southwest Virginia, Tennessee or West Virginia live every day. I think it's in bad taste, that's all."

Byram stared at me for several seconds before he turned to Dink. "Who hired this guy?"

"Walter hired him."

Byram turned to me. The silence in the room was earsplitting. "And how long have you been working here young man?"

"About six hours now. Sir." I've made $24, I thought to myself.

"I see, and just because I have been here since this was a tobacco field in 1949 you know more about theme park development and marketing than I do with your six hours experience."

"Well, it has been an eventful six hours, Mr. Hutton."

My joke seemed to break the tension, but Byram never smiled. He made a few more general announcements with no more interruptions from me or anyone else, then cut it short since it was an operating day.

I ducked out the door without being seen and walked briskly back down the hallway. Just as I turned the corner, I came face to face with the Craft-Tech Tool guy, who seemed to be waiting for me. He backed me against the wall with that pipe in his mouth. He was an evil blue-collar Fred MacMurray.

"You changed your mind about those tools yet?"

"I told you I can't afford any tools right now."

"You can't afford not to have any," Craft-Tech guy hissed. Guys passing us only glanced and kept going. "This job requires tools. I can hook you up with a basic set of the best quality tools you will ever use. Let's see, you'll need a half- and three-eights-inch drive ratchets and sockets, metric and standard. Combination wrenches, a pair of

Channellock pliers, vice grips, a couple of screwdrivers. Metric Allen wrenches. You'll need a 22-ounce claw hammer for the coaster."

Just as I feared things were about to turn really ugly between me and the Craft-Tech guy he caught a glimpse of 10-till-2 Bill out an office window (the one where the angry bouffant was earlier) walking toward a truck holding a cup of coffee.

"There's that fat bastard," he muttered before backing away from me, like his drug deal was about to sour. "Think about what I said," he warned, watching Bill out of the corner of his eye as he started down the hall toward the door. "That set will be $355 even, broken into six easy payments. I'll be back Wednesday to get your signature." He hustled down the hall and out the door.

It was a shake-down. But he had fatter fish to fry.

After being released by the Craft-Tech guy who went outside to bag Bill, I also walked down the hall and out the door, a little uneasy about my encounters with Byram in the meeting and now the Craft-Tech guy in the hall. I ran into Mudflap, Lump, Barnyard and some of the other guys I had not yet met.

"You're tangling with big enemies," Mudflap remarked to me. "First Wink, then Craft-Tech, now Byram."

I shrugged. "Yea, well. Whatever."

"You know," Mudflap continued, "Byram worked as a field hand for the farmer that owned this property back in the 1940's. One of the agreements the farmer made when he sold the property to the Peterson family to build the park was that Byram have a job for life because the farmer thought he was retarded. He can't be fired no matter how stupid his ideas. But he sure as hell can fire you."

"How did he rise into such an important job then?" I asked. I then suspected the Peter Principle, which I had studied – competent employees in management are promoted, but eventually into positions where they are incompetent. They then remain in those positions because they cannot demonstrate any further competence that would get them promoted any more.

"He's a figurehead," Bill confirmed my hypothesis as he entered from outside. He was really good at avoiding the Craft-Tech guy. "He deals only in high-hat ideas. By the time his ideas get around to being built they're nothing like his original idea."

"Hey I just encountered the Craft-Tech guy in the hall, Bill."

"Rooty patootie." Bill hustled back out the big door. For such a big guy he was damn nimble.

Remember the clown booth, somebody asked. Wasn't that Byram's idea?

"Yea, yea," Mudflap recalled. "We built a clown dunking booth five or six years ago. He hired this comedian to sit on a tractor seat over a dunking tank while people paid $5 to throw three baseballs at a paddle. He would toss out insults to taunt the thrower and make them buy more balls. Then a bunch of people complained.

"About what?" I asked.

"Byram had the sign shop make a disclaimer. It said something like 'this is satire humor' – 'the management of Burkewood Fun Park is not responsible for insulting comments made by the clown,' something like that. Made us look like idiots."

"Remember too," Wade added, "that some pro baseball pitcher nailed the paddle all three times and it never dunked the clown. That's when it was revealed the game was rigged – on Byram's instructions."

Mudflap laughed. "We cut it up with torches on a court order after that."

"But you would think he learned his lesson about monkeys," Wade continued.

Everybody laughed. "No shit," Mudflap crowed. "Especially after Monkey Island!"

"What was Monkey Island?"

"About ten years ago Ford Lake was twice as big as it is now and had a man-made island in the middle," Barnyard explained. "Byram wanted to do something with that island, so he had an idea to build these cement trees and cages and tire swings and shit then put a bunch of monkeys on it and call it Monkey Island. He claimed people would enjoy watching the monkeys play on that island while they sat on the patio and ate their corn dogs and rubber pizza. So, we spent months building all this stuff out of concrete all over this island and they brought in these monkeys from somewhere."

I was intrigued. "What kind of monkeys were they?"

"I don't know they had these big red asses. Anyway, they invited the local newspaper and radio station guy out here and they made a big deal out of floating these cages of red ass monkeys out on the island and turning them loose. They lasted maybe three minutes on the island."

"Why?"

"Fucking monkeys can swim. Nobody thought to ask. After three minutes all these monkeys were swimming away from the cement city we spent all winter building. They reached land and scattered. All we saw was red asses and hairy elbows. Picture on the front page of the paper was all these monkeys running away. I forget what the headline said."

"They couldn't find them all," Mudflap clarified. "That's why they had to bring in Harry."

"Oh yea, 'happy Harry.' Harry was this fat-jowled guy whose mouth hung open all the time but was a hell of a shot with a .22 rifle. He used to shoot copperheads down on that water ride that they tore down after that guest got bit. Anyway, they brought in Harry with his rifle because they couldn't catch about ten of those monkeys."

"Wait ..." I could not believe what I was hearing. "They brought in Harry to actually shoot and kill the monkeys?"

"No, tranquilizer darts, but a bunch of them got killed anyway," Wade added. "Harry would shoot them wherever he happened to see them. He saw one scampering across the Gator track, and when he shot it, it fell about seventy feet, killing it. I don't remember the headline but I remember they ran a picture of Byram and the caption was a joke from a TV show that said, 'As God is my witness, I did not know monkeys could swim.'"

"WKRP in Cincinnati," I added. "It was an episode about a Thanksgiving promotion where they threw turkeys out of a helicopter. I loved that show."

"Yea, that was it," Wade continued. "The park was thankfully closed so Harry just walked around with his rifle. He could spot one of those red ass monkeys in a tree or on a ride from 150 yards away. He found one eating sandwiches in a concession stand, and even cornered one in a restroom. He would aim for its shoulder or haunches and pull. Pow! That monkey would drop like a bridesmaid's dress."

I was still stunned. "My God I can't believe that."

"Rumor has it three or four of those monkeys are still roaming around the park somewhere. We've heard complaints from people saying they swore they saw a monkey looking at them through a bathroom window. Remember when that elephant died?"

"Wait ... the park had elephants?" I asked, trying to resolve this overlap of bizarre stories. "I don't remember ..."

"Just one," Mudflap interrupted. "He was a million years old. People paid $2 to ride him while he walked around in a circle. One day he was carrying Miss Virginia and he just stopped, laid down and died. Almost squashed Miss Virginia. AC and refrigeration guys dumped trash cans full of ice on him until a guy came down from DC to do the autopsy. He got out of a rental car carrying a briefcase and a chainsaw. That's when I got the hell away from there. Damn shame."

First copperheads, then red ass monkeys, then elephants, now we're threatening turtles. This place is hell for animals.

Chapter 11: in which I get my red ass handed to me

SUDDENLY BYRAM EMERGED out of the office hall door and the crowd dispersed. He put his hands on his hips and stared at me. He didn't need to say a word.

I briefly hesitated then walked slowly over to him. It was go time. I guess Harley Race was going to escort me out by the arm next so I could take that long ride home talking to myself.

"Just so you know," he started, "I don't appreciate being embarrassed in front of the entire maintenance staff."

"I understand, Mr. Hutton, It was a reaction, not an attempt to embarrass ..."

"Stop talking." Byram's voice was suddenly sharp and loud, like a thunderclap. "I can appreciate anyone's concerns about our plans but if they have anything to say they do it in a more confidential and more professional manner. Unlike what you did. You're just a maintenance flunky and you have to learn to accept that I know what is best for you and this park."

Ouch, damn.

"I don't know what I was thinking," I muttered apologetically, wanting this over ASAP. "It just kind of came out."

"Diarrhea just kind of comes out."

Good one, Byram. "Yes sir."

He raised a bony finger at me. It looked seven inches long. "I don't want to hear or see any more from you the remainder of your career here, whether it's one day, or one year, or a lifetime."

I thought of Lloyd the guard and his heart-stopping thirty years. "Yes sir."

"Because I deserve respect. I've been here since this was a cornfield."

"I thought it was a tobacco field, sir."

"I dropped out of high school in the eighth grade and worked my butt off to get where I am." His voice was rising in pitch and intensity. He was making himself angrier. "I am proof that nobody needs a fancy college degree to be successful."

My only choice was to let him bluster. He obviously needed the self-validation. "I'm impressed sir."

"As you should be. You maintenance guys will always be maintenance guys. Bottom of the chart. None of you will ever achieve my position in the company. You will never attain the status I have at this park. You saw where I am in the organizational chart – I'm third from the top."

Okay, the conversation had peaked and now was spiraling in a bizarre downhill crash and burn.

"I see maintenance guys like you come and go all the time but I'm still here, near the top. Guys like you don't plan – you only turn a wrench, you know what I mean?"

"I'm not sure I follow ..."

"What education do you have young man?"

"I graduated college a couple months ago with a ..."

"I didn't know they offered college degrees in turning a wrench. Did you minor in disrespect too?"

"Excuse me? Mr. Hutton, I told you I ..."

"What did this degree get you?" He was now pummeling me with a digressive fusillade of insults. He had nothing left to say but he was saying it anyway. "You're not a mover or a shaker, you're a college punk turning a wrench for four dollars an hour. That's all your college got you. Four years and thousands of dollars down the toilet. Turning a fucking wrench. Your parents gotta be proud."

"I hardly think that ..."

He folded his thin white arms again. "How many jobs did you apply for before applying here?"

"I don't know – dozens, I guess. Good jobs are hard to find."

"Damn right." He pointed again at me. "And that proves we hire anybody. You got turned down by everybody but we hired you. And I don't think you appreciate that. Your degree got you nothing, college boy."

I wanted to be furious and tell this son of a bitch off, but I couldn't. He was knocking me out. He knew what he was doing. I started to speak but my voice was weak and faltering, my reasoning muddled. This never happened in college. "I can't say for sure that ..."

As my voice and argument faded, Byram's just got stronger, louder and more commanding. "I dropped out of school in the seventh grade to manage a farm. Then when the park bought the property, I came to work. They saw my talents and work ethic and they hired me on the spot. I have been managing the rides operation and maintenance and planning since 1950. I didn't need no college to be a success. Nobody does. Leadership is something you have to be born with. It's not nothing you learn sitting in a class."

"... I heard you were guaranteed a job for life. Sir."

"Life has no guarantees young man. Hard work and respect is the only guarantee."

Good non-sequitur, Sir.

"And you need to toe the line if you expect to keep this job, even though it's just turning a wrench."

"Okay." I was starting to tremble. I was not taking this as well as I thought I could.

And he wouldn't fucking stop. I was prone on the mat and he had me by the throat with one hand and was still punching with the other. "We hired you out of the goodness of our hearts but we don't have to keep you. The maintenance ship is leaving port and if you want to be on it, you'll shut your mouth and see and do things my way."

"Yes sir." Please don't start killing me with corporate clichés also. I felt two inches tall.

"Alright but now I'm paying you an hourly wage to turn a wrench so get back to work.

"Yes sir."

"Put that sheepskin to good use, college boy."

"Right away sir."

Fifteen minutes. I just made a dollar getting my red ass handed to me.

Chapter 12: in which things go from bad to much, much worse

I WAS SO ANGRY, EXHAUSTED AND DISCOURAGED from my encounter with Byram that I had to go back in the break room and sit down to stop shaking. I realized I had some maturing to do.

This was no more the care-free college life. I was no longer protected by the university's ivy-covered institutional protocols when I confronted a campus cop, or got up in a professor or fellow student's face to pontificate on some shrill philosophical or political ethos that I espoused. Nothing was black and white anymore – this was the real world, where pin-headed morons sometimes ordered you around, with all the brutality and the unfairness that is baked into it and you do what they say and you can't do a damn thing about it.

And what exactly were my options about what just happened? Ordinarily, an employee could go to his human resource director to complain about poor treatment at the hands of another officer of the company, right? But I had pissed that one off as well. Dink hated me too. I had no options, nowhere to turn.

Wink and Dink. That just occurred to me.

Entering the break room, I noticed Merv, the communist-hating free slaw and potato salad guy continuing his lunch. Only he wasn't eating, he was just sitting there, looking down at his food, which included a half-eaten bowl of his own free potato salad.

I sat down at the table closest to the door, leaned back against the wall and closed my eyes. I was as mad at myself as I was at Byram. I couldn't tell if I wanted to quit or just die. I reminded myself this was the working world, and my need for a paycheck had to override my anger at a boss.

I opened one eye then closed it when Barnyard came into the lunch room. "If you're waiting for free fruit it ain't coming."

"You never know what's coming," I claimed, without opening my eyes.

"What's the matter, Merv, you look like you saw a ghost," I heard Barnyard say. *Snock.*

"Did anybody else eat this cole slaw or potato salad?"

"Just everybody. Why?"

"It ain't no good." I opened my eyes to look at Merv. He was pallid, like he needed to throw up but couldn't. I smiled in satisfaction that I didn't eat any of his dumpster finds.

Barnyard washed out his thermos while looking concerned at Merv. "What do you mean? How do you know it's bad?"

"Oh, it's bad," Merv moaned. "I could tell after I ate a bunch of it. I'm not right. I'm burpin' up bad stuff."

"Well I ate it, and it didn't taste bad to me," Barnyard argued, suddenly alarmed for the very near future.

This was getting good. I watched with great amusement the two of them try to talk each other out of being food poisoned. The more Merv talked about what he was burping up, the whiter and more nervous Barnyard got. It was almost like a weird parody of Abbot and Costello. Suddenly Mudflap roared through the door on his way to the toilet.

"Damn Merv, that potato salad you fed us gave me the bratties."

"It was bad," Barnyard told him.

"No kidding."

Bill came in close behind. "Rooty patootie," he mumbled as he almost jogged to the toilet, this time not to hide from the Craft-Tech guy. I had to look down at his feet.

Merv informed him of the development. "The slaw was bad, Bill."

"I'm currently under that impression."

I was dying to hear the truth. "Merv, where did you really get the cole slaw and potato salad?"

"I told you," he loudly belched and made a disgusted face. "Ugh – that tasted like something dead. It came from the Tennessee Kitchen. One of the gals down there was going to throw out cases of it but it was still in date."

"If it was still in date why was she throwing it out?"

Merv fell silent – I could tell he knew something he was not telling everyone. Barnyard watched him as his lips moved.

"Merv?"

"Okay, she said that last Sunday somebody accidentally shut off the breaker to the Kitchen refrigerator and freezer. It stayed off for a week and they discovered it yesterday morning when they came in for training. Everything was warm. But they cut it back on and it got cold again. I figured it was probably okay. Maybe I was wrong."

"Oh, good God," Barnyard moaned.

Watching almost the entire maintenance department eventually file through the break room, belching and farting and in varying levels of gastro-abdominal agony from eating Merv's bad food that I did not eat, made me almost forget my encounter with Byram.

My day was suddenly a little bit better.

Suddenly Tex burst from the tool cage into the break room. I assumed he also had the runs from eating bad slaw but that was not the case.

"Jeez none of you guys are answering your radios!" he barked, out of breath. "There's a code 1 at the Gator! Life or death!"

A code what? A couple guys checked their volume buttons. Someone broke a bad wind.

"Code 1! Emergency! A Gator train jumped the tracks with people on it!"

I learned that park ride situations were coded by priority, from 4 down to 1. Code 4 for a ride meant for the person called to respond at their leisure. Code 3 meant come when you can. These were usually the codes that indicated minor or non-existent problems that were ignored by most of the mechanics. For example, an unusual squeak in a ride was usually a code 4, whereas a broken Spider spring or a clogged flipper on a Ghost River boat was a code 3.

Code 2 was a big deal. If a ride stopped unexpectedly with people on it, it was a code 2 as long as no lives were in danger. If a coaster stopped on a chain lift with people, then it was code 2. If the Wave Swinger stopped with the swings still elevated it was a code 2.

Code 1 was the true emergency. A code 1 for a ride meant the ride had stopped or crashed and lives were in danger. An actor thrown from a Scrambler bucket was a code 1. Josh washing down through the rapids ride into the pump trash screens would have been a code 1 if he were a guest. But since he was only maintenance it was more like a code 7.

And of course, a derailed roller coaster train was a big fat code 1.

Despite being deathly ill and passing lots of unpleasant flatus, all the guys stood and staggered out, most clutching their gut. It could not have been a worse time for an emergency. "Come on newbie," Mudflap shouted at me between burps as he ran to his truck, started it and stomped the gas as soon as I got in the seat. An ambulance shot by the maintenance shop toward the Gator, its siren screaming. Emergency services came to life during a code 1.

Mudflap shifted and grimaced as he sped down the service road. "Lord, my asshole's burning up."

Good to know.

A line of white maintenance trucks sped across the railroad tracks and turned skidding into the gravel road Lump had dropped me on earlier. In the daylight I could see the entire ride, unlike earlier when all I could see in the dark was an exit sign. It was huge. Ride operators in red shirts ran helter-skelter around the ride, not knowing what to do and doing nothing at all.

Mudflap roared to a stop in the gravel and jumped out. "Where's the problem!" he yelled at an operator standing fifteen overhead at the edge of the station.

The operator pointed somewhere out in the ride. "Something something the train something" he shouted not loud enough over the clatter of the lift motor.

I followed Mudflap as he bounded the station stairs. Lump and Barnyard were right behind us, farting bad slaw and salad all the way up the steps. The operators had all the guests out of the station already and they were in a panic.

"Kill the lift!" Mudflap shouted to the operators. "What happened? Where's the blue train?"

"It jumped the track after the banked curve!" a female operator who looked about twelve years old screeched at us. The lift chain finally clattered to a stop.

"Jumped the track? How do you know?"

"Jeez, look back at the back curve you can see it," she shrieked, a tear rolling down her face. "It looked like it jumped the track on one side. It's laying on its side out on the lower back curve, and its full of people!"

"Shit shit shit shit" Mudflap muttered as he ran the length of the station, hopped down on the brake zone catwalk and began jogging carefully down the catwalk out onto the ride to the back curve. A couple of other trucks zoomed to stops out under the ride somewhere. I could hear shouts out there. Sirens screamed. Radios squawked. This was bad.

"Dale you stay in the station by the phone in case I need you to go to the shop for something," Mudflap yelled as Lump followed him. Barnyard stood near me, his face white – I thought at first from the tainted foods. He belched unnaturally loud and deep. But then I thought something else was making his face white.

"Barnyard, what do you think happened?" I asked as operators ran around, phone calls were made and radios chattered.

He didn't answer. But he knew. Damn right he knew.

A maintenance guy I never saw before came walking purposefully into the station on the catwalk from out on the track. He looked just like Richard Petty, only thirty pounds skinnier and a lot angrier. His sinewy arms were covered in black grease.

"Barnyard I need to talk to you," he ordered, nervously adjusting his greasy cap.

"4-0 to 5, *scratch*."

The Richard Petty guy pulled his radio from his holster, never taking his eyes off Barnyard. "Unit 5 go ahead, Dink." He held up a finger at Barnyard to stay put.

"Can you give me a status update on that Gator train? *Scratch*."

"10-4 Dink. The left side of the train jumped the tracks just out of the banked curve over the tunnel. Seems we lost a bunch of track intermediate bolts there. The right side of the train fell down between the tracks and it slid on its running board. The brake fins cut every 4x4 intermediate in half all the way to the back curve and damaged about a dozen 4x12 ledgers. The train came to a stop on the back curve and tipped over on its side on the outside catwalk. The good news is it doesn't look like anybody's hurt real bad. The ambulance and EMTs are already here."

"How in the hell did we lose intermediate bolts? *Scratch*."

Richard Petty stared hard at Barnyard. "I'm looking into that right now."

"Base to 4-0 be advised you are 10-92, *scratch*."

My slim knowledge of radio call signs reminded me that a 10-92 was inappropriate language.

"Sorry base. 10-4. Keep me updated, *scratch*."

Richard Petty holstered his radio. "Did you walk this track today, Barnyard?"

"Yea yea," he answered, not making eye contact. He was a lying bag of crap.

"Did you notice all those intermediate bolts were gone on the left-hand side of the crown over the tunnel?"

"They were there this morning." Correction, he was a *brazen* lying bag of crap.

"So, you saw them there?"

"I didn't see any missing. *Snock*."

Richard Petty lifted his cap and scratched his head. "But it looks like they were taken out. I don't understand how they all fell *up* out of the holes instead of *down*, then vanished."

Barnyard wasn't budging. "I don't know."

"If they fell out, they would be on the ground, but they aren't on the ground."

"I don't know."

"But Barnyard, I don't understand how they got out – they have to be driven out with a hammer. They can't just fall out."

Barnyard had built an impenetrable wall between himself and Richard Petty's probing questions. But I could see him shaking. Perhaps he was starting to crack, but not yet.

"I don't know."

Frustrated, Richard Petty looked at me. "Are you Dale? Were you down here this morning?"

"Yes sir, I was."

"Is your head up your butt like Barnyard's?"

"Mr. Hutton and some guy named Wink think so, but no, sir."

"I know you're new but did you see anything on the track? Anything at all that might have looked out of place?"

I knew damn well what happened, and so did Barnyard. He had bragged to me about how strong this coaster was, of how he had been taking bolts out of the track all week just for the hell of it. And as long as they ran empty trains for maintenance and training purposes the track was fine. The weight of people in the loaded trains apparently spread the track where he removed the bolts until it hopped out, wrecking the train and causing a code 1.

"Today's my first day," I answered carefully, without lying. I was getting good at this. "I was late, and this ride appeared to be checked by the time I got here."

Barnyard appeared to almost die, both from the realization that he almost killed a trainload of guests and from the tainted slaw. He exuded even more noises and bad odors.

"Well God bless America," Richard Petty pronounced, like he had witnessed a miracle healing at a Pentecostal tent revival presided over by a preacher with two heads. "We lost fifteen one-half by eighteen-inch galvanized intermediate bolts, double-nuts and flat washers that just rose up out of their holes and walked away."

"And here's the big kick in the ass," he continued, "Nard stopped down here over an hour ago when he heard the noise and actually saw the track spreading as the train passed. He tried to get a sledgehammer to drive new bolts in to fix it, but Tex wouldn't give him one."

Richard Petty just walked away from me and Barnyard, just like he presumed those track bolts did. Barnyard was hyperventilating. He was a bad liar. He burped again, deep and flavorful. Being beside him was like living inside a Pakistani restaurant dumpster.

"I don't know what happened to those fucking bolts," he lied after Richard Petty walked down the station steps and back out toward the scene of the accident. *Snock.*

I faced him, even though I was the new guy. "Barnyard you're going to get caught sooner or later. Tell them now what you've been doing. It might mean the difference between being fired, or being arrested and convicted for sabotage, especially if someone out there is injured or dy …"

"Holy moly there Andy." He just walked away from me, unwilling to hear the truth of the shit he was in. His bumblebee ass looked drawn up in a pucker factor of at least 9.7.

Down on the ground I saw Mudflap waddling back to his truck straddle-legged, like he had just messed himself. "Damn that Merv the perv and his dumpster slaw," I heard him tell somebody. "Everybody in maintenance either got the shits or the singing lunch. Even Merv is down there on his hands and knees parking the Buick. Serves him right for giving us food he found in a dumpster."

But only I knew the truth of not just the rapids' polluted water, Josh's wild ride and the destroyed pump, but the real cause of the coaster accident and the source of Merv's tainted foods. Contrary to Byram's proclamation that I was the park idiot, I was actually the park genius – a walking encyclopedia of every dumbass incident that happened today. So far.

Mudflap laid a shop rag across the seat, got in and drove back to the shop to I guess change his pants.

I never did get to go out to the back curve to see the accident. I heard that the blue train was lying on its side on the catwalk like a big dead caterpillar. Luckily, so I understand, the lap bars kept the people in their seats so none got thrown out. The injuries were relatively minor – bumps and bruises. But the damage was catastrophic.

The brake fin on a coaster is a thin flat steel plate extending vertically across the middle bottom of the train, from front to back. Every other car had one. When the train hopped out of the track on one side the other dropped down, and the steel brake fin acted like a knife blade, slicing through and cracking the 4x12 ledger boards that hold the track and shattering over one hundred 4x4 intermediate boards that keep the track properly spaced. The more intermediates that got broken the farther apart the track spread. Richard Petty said if the train had gone another fifty feet it would have dropped straight down through the structure to the ground. And most likely killed everyone onboard.

Since the boom truck was still ass-end down in the rapids ride reservoir, Dink had to call in a bucket truck from the local electric co-op to get the guests out of the Gator train and down to the ground. I did not get to participate in this evacuation.

I had to go fix Bump'em cars.

Chapter 13: in which I learn about Bump'em cars, girl-watching and Barnyard's "problem"

AFTER HANGING AROUND the Gator station for an hour doing nothing and earning four dollars, the Richard Petty guy told Barnyard to just return to the shop and to take me with him. Our assistance was not wanted in the evacuation process. Worse, I was being lumped into the same category as a ride saboteur.

I needed to put some distance between me and Barnyard.

Byram had driven by the Gator station in his own sparkling personalized F-350 diesel dually park pickup truck and had seen me and Barnyard in the station doing nothing. That's why we had to leave.

"4-0 to 3-6, *scratch*."

"Oh crap." Barnyard pulled out his radio then paused. "Should I answer?"

"You better."

"He might be calling to fire me."

"That very well may be," I acknowledged. "You still better answer."

He held the radio to his mouth and winced. "3-6 go ahead."

"Take that new guy down to the Bump'em cars," Dink ordered. "Tex called and said they had five cars down. We have several rides down but that ride is packed and they need all the cars they can get. *Scratch*."

"10-4." He holstered the radio. "Well me and you are goin' to the Bump'em cars. That's it – the last place they send you before they fire you."

"They probably don't want you at the Gator anyway," I speculated. "That Richard Petty guy thinks you sabotaged the ride."

Barnyard was quiet for a minute, looking like he was either lost in thought or was getting ready to puke. For the first time he looked me in the eye and spoke honestly.

"I do not sabotage rides," he explained with a sincerity I had not heard yet from him. "I was going to be the hero. I was going to take out a bunch of bolts then one day scatter them on the ground and say 'look here, I found all these bolts that fell out.' George, Merv and Dink think I'm an idiot but I'm not. I'm a good mechanic."

"Setting up a ride to crash intentionally is no way to prove you're not an idiot."

"I didn't mean for it to crash I was going to do it tomorrow I swear," Barnyard scrambled to answer. "I never crashed a ride. I was going to find the bolts and we'd put them back in and Dink would say good job Barnyard, you found that problem and saved guests' lives. I just needed it to run one day with guests on it, just one damn day. Who knew the ride would crash on opening fucking day. Fuck."

"I take it you've done this before."

I guessed that nearly killing a trainload of people made Barnyard want to cleanse himself of the guilt he carried. "I loosened a hydraulic line once on the Wave Swinger brakes then found it just before the ride opened," he confessed. "I've taken cotter keys out of coaster running wheels then announced what I found. One time I pulled bolts from the old-style mutton-leg brakes on the Black Racer coaster when it was still here then called Dink to tell him. He congratulated me for my good eye. Said the train would have crashed if I hadn't found it. It's all about job security."

My partner was a slave to praise from management and was willing to risk life and limb to get it. Other people's lives and limbs, not his own.

"You know you'll probably eventually get questioned about whether you walked the Gator track."

"I don't worry about being questioned. I've been questioned before, but you can't tell nobody about this,"

Barnyard warned as he drove down the service road before parking behind a closed food stand behind Plaza Americana, a short distance from the Spider. "This is the first time anybody got hurt. It won't happen again."

"Besides," he added as we got out of the truck, "I walked the track before you got there this morning."

"Liar."

"You can't prove I didn't. *Snock*. Holy moly there Andy!"

Well, he seemed back to his old self. "You're not supposed to say that anymore."

He dropped the truck tailgate and took out his five-gallon toolbox and we entered the plaza through a hidden gate behind a Whack-a-mole game that was being worked on by a young technician. He was holding a hornet's nest of colored wires and looked like he didn't know what to do with them. Barnyard told me to carry his tool bucket, so I did.

We were suddenly immersed in an old timey amusement experience, with carny music and game barkers hawking business and the roar and clatter of the older model flat rides reminiscent of the boardwalk parks of the early twentieth century. The air reeked of spun sugar, syrupy carbonated drinks and fried sausages. The backstage horrors I witnessed today temporarily faded from memory.

The plaza crowd was sparse, with nowhere near what a broiling August day brought. The precious few who walked aimlessly from one closed ride to the other were bundled in sweatshirts and coats. Some wore blaze orange raingear in case there was another cloudburst.

As we walked to the Bump'em cars building, Barnyard belched loud and open-mouthed, earning disgusted looks from a nearby couple.

I heard the woman mutter "Hogs grunt and don't say excuse me."

"I'm starting to feel better," Barnyard announced. Then, to my disgust and others around us, he silently dragged rotten eggs all the way to the ride.

"Your voice has changed but your breath smells the same."

"Holy moly there Andy!"

"You're not supposed to say that anymore."

"I'll say what I want there, Andy!"

We passed the Bump'em car building and saw the long line. The ride had thirty cars total, and five were parked all the way in the back, tied off with trash bags. The riders were driving in a counterclockwise direction, bumping and banging into one another. The stink of graphite and burnt electricity from the overhead electric grid hung in the air like charred microwave popcorn.

The Bump'em repair shed in the back of the building was split and shared with a water-skiing show that performed three days a week on Ford Lake in July and August.

Barnyard and I walked to the rear of the building and into a maintenance area. "This is 10-till-2's kingdom," he informed me. "Him and sometimes Merv camp out here all day in the summer."

The shop had a workbench, a drill press, a cable hoist and the all-important refrigerator. At the far wall was a storage closet with an unlocked padlock hanging on the hasp. I failed to see the appeal – there was nothing there to make me want to hang around all day.

I dropped Barnyard's tool bucket as he opened a large door to the ride floor, introducing the sounds of the Bump'em ride into our cold, industrial and lifeless shop. When the cycle stopped, he motioned to the operator and she held the line while he and I went onto the floor and pushed one of the broken cars into the maintenance area, closing the door behind us.

"Please exit from your car and walk, don't run to the exit," the operator instructed in a tired monotone on the loudspeaker. "Enjoy the rest of your day at Burkewood Fun Park, where there's fun around every corner."

"Usually it's the wiring in the motor," Barnyard explained of his troubleshooting process as he hooked the cable hoist under one side of the car. "Crank 'er up."

"Welcome to the Bump'em Cars, next group hop in your cars and place your arm through the seat belt," the operator yawned to the next group of riders. "Enjoy your ride."

I cranked and the car rose on one side of its rubber tube, exposing the bottom. A Bump'em car motor is under the center front of the vehicle and has a rubber tire that encircles it. Two rear steel wheels act as grounds, and power is provided by the overhead grid. The long arm on the back of the car is called a stinger, and rubs against the grid to drive the motor. The car is basically a grounded electrical generator.

"I don't see anything wrong with it," Barnyard dismissed after a cursory look. Everything on the bottom of that car was coated in black graphite dust. "Crank it back down."

I cranked it down and Barnyard unhooked and shoved it down to the far end of the shed. He opened the door to get another one. He wasn't even going to try to fix it.

The second one we pushed in had a flat rubber tube. "Damn flat tire," Barnyard sighed. "They're a bitch to change. It takes all day and you pinch the tube every time. We'll get night shift to change it." He also rolled this one down beside the other one.

Barnyard really did suck as a mechanic and he was lazy as sin. No wonder he needed to sabotage rides to look good for the bosses. He seemed to have zero mechanical skills.

The next car was so obviously broken that even I found it – the steering wheel was missing. "Run back yonder in the parts closet and get another one," Barnyard requested as he watched the crowd standing in line.

"Welcome to the Bump'em Cars ..."

I went back in the closet and fumbled for the light switch. The door was on a spring and self-closed, sealing me in the dark. As I fumbled in the blackness for a wall switch, I noticed a beam of light shining through a hole under a shelf. Without finding the light I curiously walked over and looked through a dime-size opening.

I observed a comfy pink room with a wall of mirrors on one side and a set of lockers on the other. A bench ran through the center of the room. A sign on the far wall said "do not throw sanitary napkins in the toilet." Good grief, I was looking into the water-skiing show girl's dressing room. No wonder Bill and Merv camped down there all day during the summer.

I found a light switch and a steering wheel and carried it back out into the dreary Bump'em car shop. I popped the wheel on and at the next cycle pushed it back onto the floor. Well, one out of three got fixed.

We eventually crowded the shop with four cars, with Barnyard claiming three of them had nothing wrong with them. He stood in the big door and checked out the girls in line to ride. He claimed they weren't much to look at today, all bundled in winter clothes.

"Chicks all put their bodies away until warmer weather," he commented, gazing through the crowd. "Like that one right there." He pointed to an attractive brunette wearing a toboggan and an overcoat struggling out of her seat belt. "She probably has a great body only you can't see it." *Snock.*

"Best place to watch girls is at the Ghost River station," he added. "And at Splash Valley in the summer."

Merv and 10-till-2 would disagree with those statements.

"We had a temporary guy last summer we called Square-head," Barnyard persisted. "He could make a day just standing down there. One day they had this big cheerleading competition and the station was full of cheerleaders. He damn near broke his neck when he fell off the side of the station staring. Tried to file a worker's comp claim – he couldn't move his giant square head all weekend."

So, we have someone named Square-head falling out of stations watching cheerleaders, Merv and Bill peeking at water skiing girls, and masturbating primates in Nipperville. This park was full of perverts.

Barnyard looked at me. "Did you meet Judy?"

"I did."

"What did you think?"

Trust no one. "She seemed nice."

"She's hot but I think she's a spy for Byram." Barnyard was verifying what Wade told me earlier. "You can be doing something in the shop, and look up and there she is, just staring. One night on night shift we had five code 2's in a row. Me and the others were sitting on the truck tailgate taking a break when she walked by. She smiled and waved, and looked damn good doing it. The next morning our asses were on Dink's carpet – Byram told him we were seen the night before sitting around doing nothing. Never mind we had been busting our asses for hours. I know damn well she turned us in."

Finally, Barnyard closed the big doors, announcing we were going back to the shop without fixing another car. Just before he picked up his tool bucket, he opened the freezer over the fridge.

"Holy moly there Andy!"

"You're not supposed to say that anymore."

Inside the freezer was about a hundred Styrofoam cups of single-serve ice creams. A bag of plastic spoons lay in the door shelf.

"That damn Merv and Bill, no wonder they stay down here all the time!" Barnyard exclaimed, obviously not knowing about the peep show in the parts storage room. "Look at their stash of ice cream! They must have found an unlocked freezer in one of the restaurants!"

Barnyard and I took one out and unwrapped a spoon. They were all vanilla. It was half-soft but delicious. After that one I had another one. So did Barnyard. In fact, he was so excited about the free ice cream he ate nine of them. Apparently, he was recovered from his bout with bad slaw. I stopped at four. Ice cream did not sit well on my empty stomach.

The free food benefit was again restored.

After devouring those nine cups of ice cream, Barnyard grabbed a box of spare parts off the workbench, dumped it out and filled it with ice cream containers, emptying the freezer. He wrote "eat this chumps" on the back of a blank inspection sheet and put that in the freezer instead.

I smiled, wondering briefly how Bill ate a cup of ice cream with just one hand but the thought made me a little queasy. Byram needed to throw a tarp over him and Square-head, like he did those monkeys with the blurred little hands.

"Grab my tool bucket and come on we need to find Merv and Bill."

With me carrying Barnyard's tool bucket and him carrying his precious stash of free ice cream, we walked back through the near-empty Plaza to the truck. We got in and drove around the service road back the way we came. We got stalled going around the Gator because the road was blocked by two ambulances and the bucket truck evacuating the guests from the wrecked train, so Barnyard had to back up a half mile to a turnaround and go a different way that eventually took us through the parking lot.

The parking lot was about one-eighth full. Lloyd the guard was right, hardly anybody came today. A few people walked in the biting wind from their car to the front gate to fork over $29 apiece to walk around a freezing cold park where there were no shows yet (they started Memorial Day), and half the rides weren't running.

Today was a poor investment in fun.

Chapter 14: in which I discover the real truth about park food and far too much about butts

BARNYARD AND I PARKED OUTSIDE the maintenance shop and went inside. A few guys hung around. Bill was leaning on the tool cage window chatting with Tex. I went into the lunch room, spotted Walter's sandwich and continued into the bathroom. I wondered if I would ever see the guy who hired me and owned that sandwich.

When I came out Mudflap and Barnyard were taking a break at one of the tables.

"Did you hear the news?" Mudflap asked.

"What news?" Bill asked as he entered the break room trying to tear open a honey bun, probably bought for nine cents at Price Club. Now I could only picture him in the closet peeking through that hole, his feet at 10-till-2, sweat beads on his forehead, muttering rooty patootie.

"Seems the entire group sales and marketing departments think they all got food poisoning from those damn deli trays."

"The one Wink brought in?" Barnyard asked.

I was vindicated. "You guys should be thanking me for getting that toxic food taken away," I announced with a long-overdue sense of self-satisfaction.

"I heard those women in marketing were puking in their desk trash cans."

"Damn I wished I worked over in marketing," Barnyard recounted as he shuffled a deck of cards. I'd love to work around those hot chicks." *Snock.*

I'm sure they would love having you around, Barnyard.

Lump entered the break room, still fighting the after-effects of Merv's bad salad. He was white and shaky and only stared straight ahead.

We were all walking a tightrope of noxious food and fragile employment.

Barnyard started laughing at him. "My titties stay black and blue all the time!"

Lump was too sick and weak to respond. He bee-lined straight for the toilet.

"It ain't just bad deli trays," Bill asserted. He had the inside scoop on all the park food. "It's most of the food in the park that was kept in the main refrigerator and freezer at the Tennessee Kitchen. It accidentally got cut off for a week. They think everything thawed then re-cooled sometime last week. People are sick all over the park, employees and guests."

"Merv admitted to me earlier that's where the slaw and potato salad came from," I added, not worrying about any blowback – because why should I? "A young lady down there was throwing it in a dumpster but Merv took it anyway."

"Ah-hah." Mudflap patted his aching belly and shook his head sadly. "That's why I saw Wink a few minutes ago blowing his guts outside of his fancy office."

Barnyard started a game of solitaire. "Better out of the attic than out of the basement."

I decided to change the subject and go fishing, in a manner of speaking, to see if I could hook me a horny, big-ass Bill. "Does anybody know when the ski show starts up?"

Bill bit, just like I planned. "July 4th weekend," he noted with authority. "Then two shows a day every Thursday, Friday and Saturday until Labor Day. They start practicing daily June 15, from around 10:00 in the morning until 3:00 in the afternoon. It's a great show, I try not to miss it."

I put on my most sincere face. "What time do the skiers have to show up to the dressing rooms?"

"Around 9:15 or 9:30 on those mornings. Why?"

A horrible muted rasping noise emanated from the bathroom, followed by a moan and a courtesy flush. Poor Lump was dying a slow death in there.

Barnyard scooped up his game and shuffled the deck again as he looked at the bathroom door. "I don't know what was inside Lump, but it's coming out a-hollerin'."

"I was just curious," I answered Bill. "I know a girl in college who's thinking about being a skier. She's a gymnast and a cheerleader, about 19, black hair and athletic. She would be good at it."

I saw Bill's eyebrows jump. He was on my hook. "She your girlfriend?"

"No, I think she might be a lesbian, or maybe bisexual." I hooked him good and was reeling him in. I could almost see the sweat droplets on his forehead.

"Are you sure? How do you know?" He was practically panting.

I thought and picked my words perfectly. "She always said she would rather be around beautiful, athletic girls than boys. She's an instigator – whenever she's in a group of girls at the sorority house she was always stripping to her panties to start a tickle fight, or a game of naked Twister." I shrugged. "I don't know."

"Sweet Jesus." Bill sputtered, looking as if he was going to explode. "Have you ever seen the ski show?"

"I haven't seen as much as you have." I had the biggest prize-winning fish in the lake in my boat, flopping.

Barnyard was laying out a game of solitaire. "Hey 10-till-2, the Craft-Tech guy is out in the shop."

"Dammit!" Bill's fantasy bubble burst and when he stood to run into the bathroom, Barnyard gave himself away by busting out laughing.

"Damn Bill! I'm just shittin' with ya!"

Bill sat back down. "That's not funny."

Barnyard laughed again. "That guy have pictures of you naked?"

Gosh, that would be ironic. But I threw him back. Catch and release.

Something suddenly dawned on me – when the Craft-Tech guy had Bill cornered in the toilet stall during lunch, he said something about if he "wanted to keep working on the Bump'em cars" he better pay. I didn't understand at the time, but apparently the Craft-Tech guy knew about Bill's peephole in the water ski girls dressing room. That crafty bastard was shaking Bill down – no wonder he got a 2,000-piece tool set out of him.

Lump drifted out of the bathroom, a bleached and partially-deflated Macy's Thanksgiving Day balloon. His pants were unbuckled and he held them in place with one hand. I held my breath, remembering how he got his nickname and wondered what he was going to do.

"You gonna survive, Lump?" Mudflap asked. "Looks like you came out before you were finished."

"Something ain't right," Lump answered, his face a pained knot.

Oh no. More butt talk.

Lump suddenly turned and dropped his pants to his knees, exposing a pair of striped boxers. I winced and prepared for the full monty, but it didn't happen, thank God. "You see any blood on my drawers, Mudflap?"

I turned away. How did we go from naked Twister to Lump's bleeding hemorrhoid?

"We've been through this before, Lump, but I don't see any blood this time."

Barnyard couldn't let that one go. "I don't see any blood but I see two black and blue titties." *Snock.*

"It ain't a hemorrhoid really it's more like a gut," Lump groaned as he raised his pants and buckled them. "That damn cole slaw."

Unable to take any more talk about hemorrhoids, guts or anything else butt-related, I was about to walk back out into the maintenance shop when slaw-stealing, communist-hating Merv walked in. He was soaking wet except for his dyed, wavy hair, which looked perfect. He sat down at the table closest to the door.

"I feel a little bit better."

"How's the evacuation of the Gator going Merv," Bill asked. Since the conversation was veering away from guts and lumps, I decided to sit back down.

"They about got everybody out. After evacuations, Dink said we got to go down there and take the train off the track and bring it in here."

"How we going to do that?" Mudflap asked. "The boom truck is still in the rapids reservoir."

Barnyard scooped up his losing solitaire game and started shuffling the cards. "Hey Merv, had any good ice cream lately?"

Merv looked curious. "Ice cream? Why?"

Barnyard walked out of the lunch room. A minute later he came back carrying his box. "Here ya go boys!" He grandly announced, setting a cup of the melted ice cream cups in front of the guys.

"What's this?"

"Free ice cream! All you want!"

Merv looked at his cup. "Hey, wait a minute – where'd this come from?"

Barnyard was laughing. "Where do you think it came from?" *Snock.*

While examining his cup, Bill came to enraged life. "You SOB! You were down in the Bump'em car shed, weren't you?"

Barnyard tapped his nose and laughed again. "Way to go Sherlock, you cracked that one wide open!"

Merv stood, threw his in the trash harder than he needed to and stormed out of the break room. He turned and went straight down the hall to Dink's office. "That's the last straw Barnyard!" Bill snarled, his face turning red. "Your ass is going to hang out to dry over this!"

"Holy moly there Andy!" Barnyard wasn't scared. He knew the ice cream was stolen. Merv and Bill couldn't make the case.

Mudflap opened his cup and it was milk. He chunked it in the trash.

Lump threw his away without even looking at it.

A few minutes later Merv came back in the lunch room. His face was as white as his stolen ice cream that he complained had been stolen from him. Apparently, when he told Dink that Barnyard pilfered their ice cream, Dink asked him where he got it. Rather than admit he and his crew stole it from a food service freezer, he walked out.

"What's the matter Merv?" Barnyard was laughing himself stupid. Well, more than usual. *Snock*. "Did you solve the mystery of the stolen ice cream? Get to the bottom of it? Are heads going to roll?"

Merv stormed out of the break room, followed by Bill and Lump. I also got up to leave, leaving Barnyard laughing at the table by himself.

This chapter was over.

Bill nudged me as we were leaving. "Tell your lady friend to come on out and audition for the ski show. I'd love to see her."

I'll bet you would.

Chapter 15: in which I witness a most painful series of events

AFTER BREAK I WAS HANGING OUT with a bunch of guys by the tool cage window when the Richard Petty guy came in from outside. He looked filthy and exhausted.

"Dale, Loss Prevention has the Gator evacuation pretty much under control and I can't do anything until all the people are out, so how about you go with me down to the Carousel and we spray that disk brake? It's squealing pretty bad."

This was an example of a Code 4. "Sure."

I got in the truck with the Richard Petty guy and we drove down the back side of the park near the Bump'em cars.

"I didn't mean to put you on the spot at the Gator in front of Barnyard earlier," the Richard Petty guy admitted. "I know Barnyard does stuff to rides to make himself look better. I just can't catch him, and until today there wasn't any fallout to his shit."

"I understand."

"Dink wants to fire him over this Gator crash but so far I can't pin anything on him. I'm 100 percent sure he took out those bolts in the track, but I'm only 10 percent sure of what weird experiment he was doing." He looked straight at me. "Confidentially, did he say anything to you? It won't leave this truck, I promise."

How was I supposed to answer that? Should I respect the confidentiality of my fellow maintenance employee, who confided in me how he was guaranteeing himself job security? Would it be right for me to place his job in jeopardy by revealing his scheme?

Oh, hell yes. Barnyard was a terrible person and a threat to this park and everyone in it. "He admitted everything to me," I disclosed. "The Gator bolts, a Wave Swinger brake hose, coaster wheels cotter keys, and the coaster brake mutton leg bolts. He admitted to all of them. He is a terrible mechanic, a liar, a thief and the laziest and most obnoxious person I ever met. He's guilty as sin and he will eventually get people killed. He said he was going to let the ride operate one day then 'find' the missing bolts. He is a slave to management praise and will stop at nothing to get it."

Richard Petty stared out the windshield silently for a good minute as he pulled the truck around the back of a games booth. "Anyway, he drawled, "all that rain we got makes the Carousel stop really slow. It is one of the only Philadelphia Toboggan Carousels still operating that has the original old friction drive."

Um, okay. I couldn't help but wonder how much he truly wanted to catch and punish Barnyard. "How does the friction drive work?"

"There are facing electric motors that drive two rawhide cones," Richard Petty explained. "When the operator pushes the lever forward it lowers the drive disk onto the cones. The drive disk turns a shaft that runs the big bull gear at the top that rotates the ride. At the end of the cycle the operator pulls the lever back and the disk raises against two brake pads that skids it to a stop. If water or grease drips on the disk it squeals like a pig and it takes too long to stop."

I was intrigued. "What do we do?"

"Just spray some alcohol-based solvent on the disk to clean and dry it," Richard Petty explained as he pulled into a parking spot. "We can do it between cycles without stopping the ride."

We got out and walked across the Plaza Americana over to the Carousel in between a handful of people still bundled against the forty-degree temperature and biting wind. The alcohol-soaked contractor was long gone.

The Carousel was one of those really old fancy Philadelphia Toboggan models, with a row of sixteen horses called "standers" on the outside and two rows of forty "jumpers" on the inside. The ride was loading as we got there, so we went in through the exit, passed between the rows of horses across the platform and entered the octagonal drive house in the ride's center.

The center of an old Carousel is basically a huge post called a tree, with the drive unit at the bottom and the huge grease-blackened bull gear circling the top perimeter, connected by a drive shaft extending from the drive unit to a spur gear meshed with the bull gear. The entire ride is supported by the tree. Everything was covered in splatters of black grease. A recording played a loop of old Carousel music.

"Hey, how do these guys get qualified to be ride mechanics?" I asked, curious as to how an incompetent like Barnyard (and several others I observed) got his job.

The Richard Petty guy took a can of brake cleaner from a cabinet, shook it then sprayed the four-foot diameter drive disk and wiped it with a red shop rag.

"Some of the dozen or so guys in maintenance are left over from construction," he explained as he wiped. "Barnyard was hired to build the Gator, as was Nard. They both worked hacking slabs at a local lumber yard before that. Lump was a welder at the Ghost River. Some of the other guys came from different backgrounds. I know 10-till-2, or Bill, was a meat cutter at Safeway. Mudflap did maintenance at a state prison. Merv worked at a plywood manufacturing plant."

Suddenly a bell rang – the warning that the ride was about to start. I watched as the disc lowered onto the spinning rawhide cones and the entire inside shook and groaned as the ride slowly awoke. After briefly sputtering and moaning, she got up to speed. It was fascinating inside that ride to watch the combinations of shafts, cranks and gears turning. It was like being inside a watch.

"What did you do before you came here?" I shouted to Richard Petty guy over the groaning of the ride.

"I painted cars for Earl Scheib. Nobody ever came here as a trained rides mechanic," he added. "Everybody came here as something else. It's the nature of the job."

That explains a lot.

We watched the Carousel run the cycle, then after three minutes the operator pulled the outside handle, raised the disk and it slid to a quiet stop against the two brake pads. The Richard Petty guy grinned at me. "Quiet as a mouse!"

"This ride has been here since 1964, and we have never replaced a drive cone or a brake pad," he bragged. "This shit lasts forever."

We stepped outside the center house and stepped onto the ride platform to look at one of the horses. "This is Philadelphia Toboggan Carousel number 38, built in 1910," Richard Petty continued. "There are fifty-six horses, all hand-carved out of boxwood by artists in the Philadelphia area. When they arrived from a closed park in New Jersey in late 1961, they were in a million pieces, so the paint shop glued them back together and painted them. Everything on this ride is original except the wiring."

The operator rang the bell, indicating the ride was loaded (although only half-full) and was ready to go again. Richard Petty waved at the operator as she started it. The horses on either side slowly rose up then down, synchronized by those small spur gears meshed to the rotation bull gear. Soon we were at speed – much faster than it looked from the ground. It was a bit unsettling, standing on the rotating platform, and the cold air cut like a knife, but I soon adjusted to the rotation speed.

"The ride has forty jumpers and sixteen standers, and every horse but one has its mouth open," Richard Petty shouted over the roar of the ride and the carny music. "The one with its mouth shut is considered the lead horse. Every old Carousel has a lead horse. It'll have a number 1 stamped on its belly where the pole goes through it."

I looked around but could not see a closed mouth horse from where I stood.

"The ride has four chariots, 1,600 electric lights, thirty cherubs and twenty-six oil paintings," Richard Petty continued. He knew a lot about Carousels. "Originally it had a Wurlitzer self-playing organ but it blew up so we took it out and threw it away. It just plays a recording now."

Richard Petty walked to the outside of the spinning platform by a stander, and as a new guy I dutifully followed. He looked at me and grinned again as the outside world spun past in a blur.

"Watch this."

Suddenly he stepped off the moving platform onto the ground then back up on it without skipping a beat. "It's harder than it looks," he laughed. Then he stepped off again, standing in place on the ground until I rotated back around to him and he stepped effortlessly back on, right beside me.

"Did that look hard to you?"

"No," I admitted confidently. "It actually looked quite easy."

"There's a secret to stepping on and off a moving Carousel without killing yourself," Richard Petty warned ominously. "Give it a try if you think you know what it is. But good God, be careful."

I looked down at the ground. The Carousel was moving fast but not that fast. How hard could it be? Richard Petty guy stepped off and on like it was nothing.

I decided to take the plunge. Richard Petty grinned. "Don't kill yourself."

"What?"

"Aim for the fence."

What? What does he mean aim for the fence?

"I'm telling you, aim for that fence so you don't kill yourself and any guests who get in your way."

I hesitated for a second, let go of the pole beside me and effortlessly stepped off the rotating platform and the second my feet hit the ground, I launched from a cannon, full-tilt, completely out of control. I have never moved that fast, with my legs everywhere and my arms swinging wildly. I had not even begun to slow down when I collided with the metal queue-line fence that encircled the ride. I hit it so hard I catapulted off the ground and somersaulted over the railing, landing with a jarring thud on my ass on the other side. It all happened in the space of about two seconds or less.

The minute I came back to reality, I realized I was fifteen feet away from the ride, sitting down on the other side of the fence. I was surrounded by park guests, and Richard Petty was right beside me, laughing his head off as he holstered his radio.

"My God! I never saw anything in this park move that fast!" he crowed. "Are you hurt?"

I scanned my vital functions. "No, I seem to be okay," I muttered, half in shock. A crowd of park guests stood and stared at me. I was the floor show today. How embarrassing.

"Why did you jump off that ride?" a female guest asked. "Are you insane?"

Richard Petty finally stopped laughing as I struggled to my feet, dizzy and aching from my flight. He wiped his eyes and looked at the woman.

"Apparently, he doesn't know the secret."

I looked at Richard Petty, half angry and half dumbfounded. He had made it look so effortless. "Ya think?"

"That was a stupid thing to do," an older man in a black raincoat and pink rain bonnet remarked.

Thank you all for your concern.

The pink bonnet guy then pointed at my patronizing partner. "You look just like Richard Petty. The race car driver on the TV."

"Let's go," Richard Petty guy suggested to me. "During your flying exhibition I got a call from Dink. A tractor trailer full of lumber for a handicapped entry ramp arrived and we need a crew to unload it."

"So, what is the secret to stepping off a moving Carousel?" I asked.

"You'll figure it out."

Dammit.

We walked to the truck. The ride operator was laughing at me. Finally, a guest asked me if I was alright. Thank you I'm fine. I appreciate your concern. No nothing is broken.

Richard Petty guy was still snickering as we got in the pickup and drove the long way around back to the parking lot.

In a far corner by an employee entrance was an eighteen-wheeler with its back doors open. A few maintenance guys were hanging around there already, ready to unload but unable to begin without leadership. I could see Barnyard and Lump. Richard Petty drove to the truck and parked.

"Who's ram-rodding this job?" he asked as we got out.

"You are now." *Snock.*

"Well by God let's get organized."

Richard Petty did a good job organizing an assembly line. All the lumber was stacked in the front half of the trailer. We were supposed to take it all out and load it in our pickup trucks then drive it to a gate just outside Frontierville.

Barnyard hopped inside the trailer. He was going to be the guy who slid the boards down to the doors. Lump stood on a box on the ground to catch the boards Barnyard slid down to him. Lump would hand them off to Merv, then Merv to me, then me to Bill, who would stack them in a pickup.

After a few fits and starts we found our groove. The boards were twenty-foot long 2x10s, pressure-treated and heavy as sin. Barnyard picked them up, complaining with each one of how heavy they were, then with a giant heave slid them down the floor to Lump. In fact, all of us were complaining of how heavy they were.

We were a well-oiled machine, and in fact got too fast for our own good. Barnyard was sliding down one after the other without even looking when there was a glitch somewhere down the line. I think Bill dropped one, and the line had to pause – much to Lump's regret.

When the line paused, Lump caught a board and had to wait just a couple seconds. Barnyard had no idea the line paused, then grabbed and slid down another board. Lump had his hand still on the end of the previous board when the next one came sliding down.

Time stood still when we all heard the sickening pop of his fingertips getting crushed between the two boards. With no reaction, Lump dropped the board and, grabbing his smashed hand, tried to step off the box he was on. He failed – maybe he didn't know the secret – and whacked his ear on the tailgate of the truck as he fell, knocking out the cotton wad from the stethoscope incident earlier. He landed on the ground in a pile of flesh, dirty clothes and crushed fingertips and never uttered a sound.

"Jesus, Lump are you okay?" Merv more demanded than asked.

"My gosh Lump," was all I could manage. It was horrible to watch.

"Careful Lump! Jeez somebody check him," Richard Petty guy shouted.

Lump somehow struggled to his feet, yet to utter a word regarding his catastrophic multiple smashed fingers. His face was bleached white and he had kind of a dull stare in his eyes as he stood, holding his compacted fingertips with his other hand. I could almost hear them throbbing. And his ear was bleeding.

"Lump you need to get to first aid," Merv instructed.

"Lump you need to get those fingers under hot water to prevent permanent damage," Richard Petty ordered.

"No, Lump," Merv yelled, "put them under cold water. Ice water."

With his pounding right hand and his bleeding ear, Lump staggered like a zombie on autopilot across the corner of the parking lot to the closest guest bathroom while Merv and Richard Petty argued over the benefits of hot water vs. ice water for crushed fingers. Lump looked positively drunk with misery, knowing instinctually he had to do something but not exactly what. He was like a man dying of thirst looking for water, certain it was anywhere but his current location.

Merv looked at me. "Dale, follow him to make sure he doesn't hurt himself worse. And make sure he puts those fingers under cold water."

"No, hot water!" Richard Petty countered.

I tailed Lump as he staggered to the Frontierville bathroom, clutching his hammered right hand. I was a Komodo dragon tracking a wounded Wildebeest dying from blood poisoning caused by my saliva.

He wobbled through the bathroom door over to the sink as I entered, and I watched him turn on the cold water then thrust his throbbing hand under the faucet. When the ice-cold water hit his smashed fingertips, I guess the shock was too much, and as his eyes rolled up, he fainted dead away.

On his way down to the floor, he smashed his chin against the sink.

Chapter 16: in which I learn about Lump's injury history, and Byram does a most unbelievable thing

I WALKED BACK TO THE TRUCK and alerted the Richard Petty guy about Lump, who called first aid. Two EMTs came over to resuscitate Lump then carried him to the infirmary. They removed his boots for transport, so I carried them over for him, meeting them in the triage area. By that time Lump was awake but groggy.

They had to heat a pin to prick and release the pressure in every finger then bandage Lump's right hand. They put six stitches in his chin and four in his ear.

While I waited in a plastic chair in the waiting area a striking nurse with Gail on her name tag pulled Lump's file and sat beside me to ask me a few questions about the accident. Lump's file was six file folders and massive.

An enormous EMT with a jiggling gut, a porn mustache and a thousand items hooked to his black belt passed through the room and entered the main treatment area. He had so much EMT stuff hanging on him he clanked. When the door opened, I briefly saw inside that forty or fifty cots were all occupied by guests in abdominal agony that I presumed was from eating spoiled park food.

It was the Chancellorsville battlefield hospital tent.

"You look a little beat up yourself," Gail the nurse observed, looking at fresh scratches on my arm. "Are you okay?"

I looked at my battered arms. "I'm fine. I just haven't mastered the art of stepping off a moving Carousel yet."

Gail smiled. "I heard there's a secret to it."

"So I understand." This nurse was sharp. But apparently, she was not going to give away the best-kept secret in the park.

"Have you always been the nurse here?"

"Just for the last two years," she answered. "I started out as a junior in high school as a skier in the ski show. Then I decided to go into medicine."

Ski show, huh? Rooty patootie.

I watched as Gail thumbed through one accident report after another in Lump's file to get to the last one. It was an astonishing list:

- Patient got head pinned between the Ghost River station platform and a boat trying to wipe water droplets off a photocell.

- Patient hopped off a wood coaster track to dodge passing train, fracturing his shoulder blades on a cross-beam.
- Patient got struck between the eyes by a rapidly uncoiling spool of elevator lift cable, knocking him unconscious.
- Patient used his finger as a line-up tool while coupling coaster train cars, nipping the tip end off the R Index finger. It was sewn back on.
- Patient accidentally shot himself in the face with a sandblasting nozzle, filling lungs with sand.
- Patient received third-degree burn when molten torch slag dripped into his shoe.
- Patient developed a blood clot when he accidentally cut through a high-pressure pneumatic hose and was blasted in the face by pressurized air.
- Patient sustained hundreds of yellow jacket stings digging a ditch for electric cable.
- Patient received a flash burn welding. Many, many, *many* times.
- Patient fell out of the rapids ride boat trying to tighten handlebar bolts.
- Patient sustained a broken arm and numerous abrasions riding a wood coaster when the operator accidentally ran two trains together testing new brake configuration.

- Patient got vertigo and fell, injuring his back while drop-testing the observation tower elevator.
- Patient set his hair on fire welding the hitch on a dumpster.
- Patient mashed under forklift forks when a dry-rotted hydraulic line split open.
- Patient injured at a safety meeting when dry erase board fell on his head, cancelling an awards presentation.
- Patient broke ankle at Christmas party when he fell off the stage accepting a perfect attendance award.
- Patient bitten by a feral dog trying to rescue it out of the main trash compactor.
- Patient swallowed several staple gun staples.
- Patient almost crushed trying to clear boat jam in rapids ride.
- Patient sustained head injury after backing a forklift into trash compactor.
- Patient accidentally mashed by hydraulic trash cylinder trying to retrieve old refrigerator out of compactor.
- Patient injured when struck and run over by food service Cushman (loaded with strawberries?)

- Patient sprayed by skunk and temporarily blinded behind Nipperville Burgers and Fries food stand.
- Patient shot himself through cheek with Hilti gun constructing clown dunking tank.
- Patient shot himself through scrotum with Hilti gun while constructing Monkey Island.
- Patient nailed his own hand to the side of the guess-your-name game with Hilti gun. Sustained further injury when he used a crow bar to release hand himself.
- Patient treated for frostbite after accidentally welding himself inside Tennessee Kitchen meat freezer.
- Patient struck by Himalaya ride train trying to check air pressure on drive tire while ride was operating.
- Patient got foot crushed by hydraulic whip hammer while busting up concrete pad.
- Patient scalded by hotsy steam cleaner.
- While trying to repair coaster lap bar mechanism while train was in operation, patient struck head on wooden support going 62 mph.
- Patient swallowed gasoline siphoning gas out of concrete hole-saw.
- Patient accidentally ran his face through meat slicer in Frontierville Deli not once but twice attempting to plug in device.

- Patient almost asphyxiated himself with extension cord on wood coaster track when drill bit hung up.
- Patient lost fingertip replacing spring at Spider ride.
- Patient sustained multiple fractures trying to step off a moving Carousel. Glad someone else had that pleasure.

And of course,

- patient punctured eardrums playing with stethoscope at quarterly meeting.

No mention of getting treated for black and blue titties, a seemingly chronic affliction.

Gail took my statement about the accident, and told me they were sending Lump home for the day. I thanked her, considered flirting with her but changed my mind and started walking back to the parking lot to help finish unloading that truck.

But halfway there I stopped. What the hell? I was the new guy. What obligations did I have to anyone anyway? They treated me like shit all day. I had no sense of duty to them.

My thoughts turned away to more pleasant thoughts. Wonder if Gail the nurse is single? Wonder if she is dating? There was no ring on her finger. I turned and walked back to first aid. You never know unless you ask.

She was straining to return Lump's encyclopedic injury file to the cabinet when I went back in.

"Did you forget something?" she asked, almost out of breath.

"Yes, in fact I thought I would ask you something."

She sat down at her desk and turned to face me, crossing her legs. She had a sweet smile.

"We're a little busy today with the food poisoning but what can I do for you?"

I started stammering because she was sweet and approachable and I was wet, filthy, greasy and exhausted. "Well, I was wondering ... maybe over dinner you could you tell me the secret of stepping off a moving ..."

The door opened. "There you are."

It was Merv, the communist-hating, two-headed preacher quoting bad slaw-stealer with the perfect hair. I was wrong – I was indeed missed. And he came looking for me. His timing sucked. "I need you to go with me if you're through here. We have a situation with the Mississippi paddle boat in the lake and Dink wanted me to take you with me. Guests are stranded in the lake. Can you swim?"

Swim? I sighed. "Sure." Gail smiled at me. I would have to try another day.

Out in the truck Merv explained to me what happened. The Mississippi paddle boat was a well-worn, forty-passenger boat Byram bought from some defunct park in Louisiana. It was a scale replica of an old-fashioned paddle-wheel steamboat but ran on a diesel engine that could be heard all over Frontierville.

Nobody wanted anything to do with the thing but Byram insisted on taking people on scenic boat rides out on the lake. This ride was his baby. Now it was stopped dead in the water with no way to get the fifteen guests off.

Byram's ride had no contingency plan.

"We thought when Byram first got the boat that a diesel mechanic would have to ride all day on it because it wasn't in very good shape," Merv explained. "It was slow, it stunk and the diesel engine was loud and unreliable. We told Byram that if it broke down on the lake, we had no way to fix it or get the people off. None of that seemed to matter to him."

Merv looked at me with a shocked look. "And if it sinks, we are totally screwed," he added ominously. "There's no life jackets on board. I told Byram these things but he told me to mind my own business, so I shut my mouth."

We took the service road around the park and parked by the bank of Ford Lake on the edge of a concrete retaining wall near the Steel Phantom coaster. I could see the Bump'em car building and the ski show dressing areas across the lake on the other side. The paddleboat sat lifeless in the middle of the lake, listing starboard, the operator staring sadly. Fifteen pissed-off guests sat looking for a way off that stupid lake, with nothing to see but the crumbling ruins of Monkey Island.

Chunky, the skinny auto shop guy, was already standing on the bank when we arrived, staring out at that sad boat in the lake.

"Merv," Chunky asked as we got out of the truck, "how in the shit are we supposed to get out there and get that thing running again?"

Merv looked across the lake. It was almost a football field out to the boat. "Get us off this damn boat," somebody yelled.

"Chunky," Merv countered, "why is the water black around the boat?"

We all looked closely –the boat was being circled by an oily black sheen. "That would be all the diesel fuel leaking out," Chunky observed. "We're going to poison that lake with fifty gallons of diesel."

Suddenly there was a roar behind us as Byram skidded to a stop in his immaculate giant company truck. His face was crimson. "What in the name of all that is holy is going on out there," he howled through the window, Johnny Cash blasting on his tape deck.

I hear that train a-comin' ... it's rollin' round the bend ...

"The paddle boat cut off and is leaking fuel," Merv uttered in a soft voice.

"Who cut it off?" Byram demanded.

... Since I don't know when ...

We looked at each other. "Nobody," Merv answered. "Something's broken. It shut off on its own."

"Why is it leaking fuel?" Byram commanded as he got out of the truck and slammed the door just as Johnny was complaining of being stuck in Folsom Prison. "Answer me dammit!"

"We can't get out there to see. We don't know yet."

"Don't get smart with me!" Byram crackled. "We kill as much as one tadpole in that lake the county and the EPA will shut us down!"

"I'm not being smart! Merv gasped impotently. "I'm just saying that ..."

"Which of ya'll can swim?" Byram asked in the form of a shout. He was dead serious, and in the early stages of a professional meltdown. "Chunky you can swim, can't you? Skinny punk like you can probably swim like a damn fish! Swim out there with your toolbox and get that damn boat started and get those passengers back to the station!"

Chunky hesitated before trying to respond to Byram's ludicrous order. "I can swim ... but first off I might have trouble totin' a sixty-pound toolbox in thirty-foot deep water, and second I don't really want to swim through that oil slick surrounding the boat."

The black diesel plume was a good fifty feet in diameter at that point and still spreading. We could see the fuel bubbling furiously from a major break in the fuel line right at water level. Still pacing, Byram snatched his radio from his holster and started calling for Dink.

"6-0 to 4-0. 6-0 to 4-0! SIX-OH TO FOUR-OH!"

"4-0 go ahead Byram, *scratch*."

"Dinklin, the goddamn paddleboat is stranded in Ford Lake leaking fuel and none of your worthless ass mechanics will go out ..."

"Base to 6-0 be advised you are 10-92. *Scratch*."

"Screw you and your 10-92 base, this is an emergency!"

Dink came back on the radio. "Byram, can I call you on a land line? *Scratch.*"

"There's no fuckin' phone here I'm in the fuckin' lake!" Byram howled into his radio.

"Base to 6-0 please be advised you are 10-92. *Scratch.*"

Byram beat his radio repeatedly on the bed of his immaculate pickup truck out of pure frustration. Part of the mike button snapped off and danced in the truck bed.

"Are any of you assholes going to get us out of this lake, or just stand around?" a guest yelled from the boat.

"Why don't you assholes give us a fuckin' minute!" Byram screamed back at the guest, his voice breaking in panic. He suddenly looked at me, his eyes wide with terror and fear. "Hey college boy what did your fancy college classes teach you about situations like this?"

I couldn't tell if Byram was teasing me or genuinely soliciting my advice, but I elected to keep my mouth shut in either case. The guy in the boat was giving Byram the finger with both hands.

"I knew it!" Spit flew from of Byram's mouth as he pointed at me. "You got no ideas! You didn't learn shit in college! That's why I'm in charge and you just turn a wrench!"

Merv finally spoke. "You really shouldn't talk to park guests that way," he murmured, looking at the furious guy in the boat.

Never mind talking to me that way, I thought. I was watching a man and his career collapse right in front of me. And you know what? I didn't really care. This man's self-destruction was a long time coming.

But I suddenly had an idea. "Can't we bring a white-water rapids boat down here and float out to the people and bring them back?"

"Hey, that might work," Merv perked up, looking at Byram. I noticed numerous other guests had gathered on the far patio to watch this incident unfold. Some of them were eating possibly tainted food as they watched.

"Which one of your fancy college classes gave you that idea?" Byram sputtered. He again got on his radio. "6-0 to 4-0, Dink I got an idea, take out a white-water boat and bring it down here so we can get these people out of the lake."

"Uh ..." Dink came back. "No can do, Byram, we're pumping the water out of the rapids ride reservoir and can't float the boats around to the hoist. They're sitting on concrete right now, *scratch*."

Byram ramped his ballistic levels even further. "Whose lamebrain idea was it to pump the fucking water out of the ..."

"Base to 6-0 be advised you are again 10-92 and your radio privileges will be revoked for 24 hou..."

"Go to hell, base!" I noticed Byram's eyes were not focused on anything. "Dink use the boom truck to lift a boat out of the reservoir and bring it down right now!"

Dink tried to answer Byram's ridiculous demands in a level-headed manner. "Byram, remember the boom truck fell into the reservoir. We're waiting for the tow truck to get here to ..."

Galoomp. That was the sound Byram's radio made when he threw it in the lake.

"It was your idea to pump down the reservoir," I heard Dink answer on Merv' radio. "*Scratch*."

Byram was determined to resolve the problem in whatever impulsive, outlandish way he could. "Well if none of you worthless SOBs will go out and help those people and fix that boat, I'll do it myself!" He jerked open his truck door and got in.

Now Conway Twitty was serenading from his truck speakers. *"Hello darlin' ... nice to see you ..."*

Byram rolled down and looked out his truck window with crazy eyes. "When I get back, I'm firing the entire maintenance staff!" He hoarsely screamed. "Every one of you!" He roared the huge engine, put it in drive and backed the truck to face the lake. He was a man possessed.

Then, he stomped the gas and drove his perfect, F-350 park truck off the ten-foot retaining wall into the lake with a huge splash. It dove down nose first then almost immediately sank out of sight.

Everyone on the boat, those on the far bank and me, Merv and Chunky all stared in shock. We couldn't believe what just happened. It was like watching a movie. Byram actually drove his truck into the freaking lake. He was gone.

He drowned Conway Twitty.

"Hey," the guy in the boat yelled, "Aren't any of you assholes going to dive in and rescue him?"

Chapter 17: in which I reflect on my job search and ponder another job I could have had instead of this one.

I RECALLED JOB INTERVIEW NUMBER 12, the one I had just prior to the one at Burkewood Fun Park.

Three months after graduating from college and after eleven pointless and insulting interviews, I walked downtown to the Virginia Employment Commission to again look for work. The job search was going horribly, with nothing but dead ends and no offers, but I felt good that day – I was being proactive.

The Employment Commission was a grey and disheartening building, packed with people searching desperately for work of any kind. Unemployment was 11 percent in southern Virginia but 100 percent inside my apartment.

I passed through the revolving door into what looked like a cold eastern bloc post office. There was a stack of books indexed by job type and a line of a dozen people in all variations of socio-economic clothing waiting to look through them.

There was an opening for an apprentice car painter at Earl Scheib's. But I heard car painters all have lung cancer when they're forty.

There was an opening for a commissioned salesperson for Cutco Knives. I was not doing door-to-door sales with top-down commission – the boss gets rich and I starve to death.

There was an opening for a line worker in a chicken processing plant in a small nearby town. I read about this disease those people get, called chicken knots. I have my dignity.

I turned in a different book and was happily surprised to see that Bailey Advertising Company was looking for an able-bodied person to help erect billboards along Route 460.

I stared at the listing. The more I considered the job the more I could tailor it to my strengths. Finally, I was convinced I was the only person in town qualified for it.

The listing said for interested applicants to report Tuesday morning at 9:00 a.m. for an interview. Holy shit, that was tomorrow. This was divine intervention. I convinced myself I could land it. I wrote down the address.

I was so certain I had that job I stopped my search with that single prospect. I was clueless of the job search paradigm. I didn't bother with backup plans because I was twenty-two years old and knew nothing about anything.

My alarm woke me at 7:15. I rolled out of bed, took a shower, put on my cleanest clothes and drove to Bailey's, where I walked in at 8:48 a.m.

I was stunned.

A line of over 100 applicants snaked through the cavernous building's first floor, and I was at the dead end of it. I was not the lone applicant, far from it. They may as well have trumpeted this job from one of their billboards.

All of the other applicants were hungry, strapping young punks like me, just trying to secure some form of income in a terrible recessive economy.

A ramrod in khaki Dickies in the center of the warehouse shouted at us to stay in line. He was the ringmaster, and we were the performing elephants. If I missed my cue, he would take me outside and shoot me.

"Been doing construction all my life," a scab-covered bruiser in front of me turned and announced, breaking my stunned realization. Bully for him – but this was a creative job, not a construction job, wasn't it? I suddenly wasn't sure. And none of these guys looked or sounded like college graduates.

"I poured and vibrated a thousand yards of concrete in Richmond on the James Center project. Yep."

"That's swell."

"You fellas stop talking and move ahead!" the ramrod shouted to two guys about fifty spots ahead.

"Yep, I tied the rebar, set the forms, vibrated the cement ... I'm well experienced in all forms of cement applications."

His life in cement deteriorated into meaningless farting sounds. This was no highly-specialized career consultation, this was assembly-line interviewing for low-pay, bullshit grind. I was not conferring in a quiet, hip office with a young millionaire entrepreneur sporting Vuarnet sunglasses and a Members Only sport jacket with an open-collar Hugo Boss shirt. I was standing in line in a cold maintenance shop with a thousand other minimum-wage slaves just hoping, praying for a shot at anything that would bring in a few bucks.

The ramrod yelled at us to "stay against that wall" and "be quiet, dammit" like he could hear me thinking.

"Your fancy college sheepskin won't do shit for you here today!" I imagined him blustering at me. "You went to college to turn a wrench! Your parents must be so proud!"

I was finally up. I went inside a small mismatched office, followed by the ramrod. There was no chair. A bossman in a 1977 giant-collar patterned knit shirt and thick sideburns like carpet samples glued to the sides of his head sat behind a filthy desk covered in resumes. It smelled like bong water. What looked like a lawn mower engine sat broken in a corner.

He never looked up. He could have been interviewing Clint Eastwood. "Let's see a resume."

"I had no way to print one on short notice," I muttered, watching this job scurry away like cockroaches from under a hot oven. "I only heard about this late yesterday. But I did just graduate from ..."

"This is a temporary trades helper position and pays $5 an hour," 1977 bossman explained without ever looking at me. "The hours are Monday through Thursday, 7:00 a.m. to 5:30 p.m. The successful applicant will clock in every day on time, report to the site foreman and assist in digging footers, tying rebar and forming concrete pads. There may be some concrete pointing and finishing work. Reliable transportation is required, and failure to show up on time twice will result in termination. Do you have any questions about this position."

Three months ago, I was a university student with the world in front of me. Today I was standing in a bong water office, one anonymous applicant of a thousand others, competing for a dead-end construction job just to keep out of the street.

"Leave a name and phone number on this pad so we may contact you should you be the successful applicant," 1977 bossman repeated in a monotone, pushing a legal pad with dozens of names and numbers in front of me. Many were child-like scrawls, each one indistinguishable from the other.

What "successful applicant?" This guy was only collecting names.

The ramrod looked over my shoulder and watched me write the name Hugh G. Rection and a fake phone number on the pad. I did not want this job, and I wouldn't even answer the phone if he called.

Hell, I didn't even own a phone.

Sitting at a stoplight on my way home, I sadly watched a stream of filthy water from a leaking hydrant wash what was left of my career aspirations down a storm drain. My gas gauge was on empty. I was broke, hungry and dejected.

Then I saw a sign.

It was in the window of a travel agency. It was for Burkewood Fun Park, and they were hiring.

Chapter 18: in which I regretfully realized I stopped caring

I RAISED MY HEAD and looked at the wall clock. I had been waiting an hour in first aid with Merv and Chunky. We were going to talk to some woman named Morey who was supposed to be a trained psychologist or counselor or something for people like us who had witnessed traumatic events.

Gail the nurse sat at her desk in the next room, occasionally sadly looking in at us. I guess she felt sorry for us having to witness a park executive – third from the top in the organizational chart – drive his truck into a lake.

The wall clock across from me said it was 5:40 p.m. My twelfth hour on the job.

Finally, a woman in a flannel shirt, jeans and muddy boots entered in through a back door. Her brown hair was tied up in a bun. She looked as if she had been plowing a garden. "Hi Merv, hi Chunky," she greeted my co-workers.

She extended a hand to me. "My name is Morey and I am in charge of loss prevention and first aid."

She pulled up a chair across from us and sat down. "Gail could you join us?" Gail came in with a pen and a steno pad and sat down beside Morey. I was glad to have her with us. But she was somber as a funeral.

"What a day," Morey exhaled. "Just before I got the news of Mr. Hutton, I found out we got twenty dead monkeys down in that terrarium in Nipperville because some asshole threw a tarp over the air inlet, burned up the oxygen pump and suffocated every one of them. Pardon my English, Gail."

Gail shook her head sadly.

Oh God. I actually thought that news was worse than what happened to Byram.

"We got about three hundred and ten paying guests in the park and three hundred of them have the shits, as well most of the admin staff, because our main freezer got shut off all week and the food thawed," Morey continued, not mincing words. "Pardon my English Gail."

I smartly managed to avoid that plague. I smiled at my stealth-like cunning.

"Okay, a few minutes ago they recovered Mr. Hutton's body from the lake," Morey announced somberly. "Early indications are he drowned."

No fooling.

The phone rang.

Hotline, I thought. "Pardon me guys." Morey spun in her chair and answered.

"Yea? When? Oh boy. What was the cause of death? Has next of kin been ... well, what can you tell me then? Oh, okay. That's just great. Okay, bye." She hung up, turned around and remained silent for a moment.

"The actor that fell off the Scrambler last night just died in the hospital from multiple traumas. What a fucking day, pardon my English, Gail."

Gail again shook her head sadly.

"You guys may hear rumors about the recovery of Mr. Hutton from the lake," Morey explained. "I'll tell you right now what happened because I know the story will get twisted. The divers from the county placed the lifting harness under his tail end to get him out in a seated position, but in the process of maneuvering him out of the truck it slipped. When he finally came out of the water the harness unfortunately was around his neck, like he was being hanged. And, of course, the guests in the stalled boat had to witness the local electric co-op boom truck pull Mr. Hutton out of the water like that."

What a PR disaster.

Morey stared at a paper in her hand before she laid it down. "Those folks are now being taken in a church bus to a community center in town where we will have counselors available."

Morey leaned forward, placing her elbows on her knees. She looked at us with utmost seriousness. "There will be a county investigation of this incident, as well as one in-house, so let's talk now about it. You guys were the last ones to see Mr. Hutton alive. Did he give any indication to you that he was about to take his own life?"

The three of us looked at each other, each waiting for the other to speak first. "He didn't say nothing to me," Merv finally replied.

Chunky was no help either. He just shook his head no. Morey and Gail both looked at me for answers. Gail wrote something down.

Suddenly the door opened and Judy walked in. She looked remarkably stoic after losing her boss in such a bizarre manner.

"Hello Judy, please have a seat," Morey offered. She marched in and sat quietly in a chair behind us, without saying a word. "I asked Judy to join us, if that's okay."

I picked my words carefully, especially now that Judy was there – my mouth already got me in a lot of trouble today. "Mr. Hutton was freaking out over that boat being stalled and leaking fuel," I finally recalled.

"Freaking out how, Doug?"

"My name's Dale. Freaking out. Cussing on the radio. Out of control. He wanted one of us to swim with a heavy toolbox out to the boat to fix it."

"I hardly think he wanted you to actually swim out to the boat, Dale. That sounds insane."

Oh, you think?

"Yes, he did." I looked at Chunky for verification, but he only stared at the floor. Gail the nurse made more notes. I felt Judy's stony presence behind me, her eyes boring through my back. Was she pointing a gun at the back of my head? I had to tread lightly.

"Was Mr. Hutton doing or saying anything else that may have led any of you to believe he was about to perform an irrational act?"

Where do I fucking start? Everything I heard that man say and do today was irrational and crazy. He was arrogant and abusive and had no business working in a public festival environment. His ludicrous "Hootin' Holler" theme idea was a sick joke. He paraded jacking-off monkeys in front of innocent children, then killed them by throwing a tarp over their glass cage and choking off their oxygen. He ordered a rigged clown dunking tank with a disclaimer for the clown's jokes. He spent thousands of dollars corralling red-ass monkeys on an island without bothering to find out they could swim, then brought in an intellectually disabled, drooling local to tranquilize them when they escaped. He all but ordered Chunky to his own drowning death through a thirty-foot deep, diesel-polluted lake. And I'm not even including every other bullshit word that vomited from his insane, out-of-control mouth when he ate my ass up by the time clock. Jesus H. Christ, that man's entire career was stupid, irresponsible and irrational words and acts.

"No, nothing else," I shrugged. Gail wrote it down. "It's just that ..."

Here I go again. I heard Judy shuffle in her chair. What was she doing back there?

"It's just what, Dale?"

"Well, I did not get the impression Mr. Hutton drove his truck in the water to kill himself. He said if none of us would go out and help that boat, he would do it himself. I think he truly believed he could drive his truck out there and fix it."

Morey just stared, expressionless.

I don't know why I felt the need to fill the gaping chasm in the conversation. I didn't owe anybody anything. "He threatened to fire the entire maintenance staff afterward. So that tells me he was planning to come back when he was done."

"Done doing what?" Morey queried.

"Done fixing the boat."

"So, you're saying, Dale, that you were seriously under the impression, that Mr. Hutton thought he could drive his truck through thirty-foot deep water, out to the stalled boat, and fix it himself, with no tools?"

I shrugged. "It certainly seems that way."

"But that doesn't make any sense."

"No, it doesn't, does it?" I almost wanted to laugh.

Morey looked at Chunky and Merv. "How do you both feel about witnessing such a shocking act? Let's hear some feedback, guys."

I looked at my co-witnesses but they just stared at the floor. They were playing it smart.

My problem was I was having a hard time feeling any sympathy for Hutton. Yes, seeing his truck go into the water and sinking was shocking, but I just wasn't sad.

"Anybody?"

I decided to put my college English skills to some good use instead of turning a wrench because I wanted to end this entire episode.

"I am shocked and saddened by Mr. Hutton's obvious unthinking act that tragically cut him down in the prime of his career."

Morey smiled sympathetically. That was the ticket. I was laying the manure on thick. Merv and Chunky also nodded their heads in agreement.

Gail the nurse smiled sympathetically at me. She was digging my sexy line of manure.

"We all are, Doug." Morey stood. "When I hear funeral arrangements, I'll send out a memo. Thanks for your time guys, and remember my door is always open if you need to …"

Suddenly Judy jumped to her feet. "You don't understand! Mr. Hutton is not dead!" she proclaimed in a lurid voice. I briefly turned and noted her eerie smile and glassy eyes. "That was not him lifted out of the water! Mr. Hutton transcends losses that befall the rest of us! He is alive!"

Gail and Morey's mouths dropped. As did Merv and Chunky's. Not mine. I turned back around and studied my fingernails. This was nothing.

"Mr. Hutton today is seated as head of the dominion of the righteous, and he will come again to judge those who work and those who are sponges and bloodsuckers!" She wagged a finger at us. "Behold! His kingdom will have no end!"

She strode out the door triumphantly talking to herself.

And I felt nothing.

The phone rang four times before Morey could answer. "What the fuck now," she sighed as she turned to answer. "Hello? This is she ... wait, when? Jesus, is everybody okay? How the hell ... let me call you back."

Morey hung up the phone and stared at the desk for a solid minute before she looked back at me. "Well the news just keeps getting better," she exhaled. "The church bus carrying the boat riders blew a tire, ran off the road and turned over. Nobody killed but some injuries. I gotta go."

Fifteen minutes – I just made a dollar while I was losing my soul.

Chapter 19: in which I hear the final news

MERV AND CHUNKY drove park trucks back to the maintenance shop, but I elected to walk. They were in a hurry to punch out and get home. I was in no rush. I needed the decompression time.

I could hear the roars and screams from the rides as I walked back to the shop. An amusement park sounds like a weird mashup of birthday party and torture chamber. The handful of guests who were not throwing up or messing themselves were going about their fun with no idea what all was transpiring behind the scenes.

I caught a whiff of sausage from a nearby food stand and wondered if it was Lump accidentally barbecuing a body part while attempting a simple repair. A seasonal employee speeded by on a Cushman loaded with strawberries, bound for a funnel cake stand. If he tipped over and got pinned, he would be helpless as I ignored his injured ass and loaded up on free strawberries.

I wondered if the Steel Phantom coaster would simply tip over, or a Ghost River boat would explode in a ball of flame, or a Spider arm would snap and fly off into orbit, because Barnyard sabotaged it to prove what a good mechanic he was.

I thought about those guests who got stranded on a paddleboat, then witnessed a drowning, then a botched rescue, then were in a bus accident just trying to go see a damn counselor. I wondered if they would ever go to an amusement park – or even outdoors – again.

Just then, a company pickup truck with Judy behind the wheel blew past me going about sixty. Then, inexplicably, she swerved hard right and sideswiped the rear of every car parked by the building where the marketing women were puking in trash cans. I watched with a curious, detached interest as rear fenders, tail lights and chrome trim smashed, splintered and scattered as she bang-bang-banged all six cars. She then swerved hard left, never slowing down. She wiped out two directional signs and continued at breakneck speed out gate 3, steam starting to spew from under the hood.

As two marketing women took a break from puking to straggle out to see what the hell just happened to their cars, I saw the reason for Judy's erratic driving – she had swerved to miss Nard's turtle, which was in the travel lane, its head proud and high, walking toward the gate, like nothing ever happened.

Godspeed, Judy – but she wouldn't get far. In addition to a blown radiator, that truck had no license plates or inspection sticker.

I wondered about the hapless Josh, and how he had chowed down on that tainted deli and fruit tray before he was publicly chastised for picking up money and sent home. I contemplated if his mom had to stop along the highway taking him home to let him "park the Buick," as Mudflap might say.

I walked past the closed employee cafeteria. A couple of guys had the entire asphalt parking area demolished. A backhoe was dipping out huge bucketsful of rocks and dripping, stinking marl while two other guys stood watching, smoking and leaning on shovels.

Suddenly, there was a pop and a loud hiss and one of the shovel leaners yelled Gas! And he and his partner dropped their cigarettes and took off running. Apparently, the backhoe hit a gas line. The driver shut off the backhoe and jumped off in panic.

I kept walking as guys ran past me and the unmistakable rotten egg smell of gas permeated the area. Gas, they yelled, gas! But I was in no hurry to get away or even tell anybody. I was indifferent – just another disaster in a long line of them. The gas leak was of no concern to me.

I had become jaded to life after only one day at this job. I had no thoughts or memories of Burkewood Fun Park that did not include something horrific, bizarre, stupid or deadly. I was dead inside. The threat of obliteration by leaking gas made me yawn. I would love some of those strawberries.

It took the park only 12 hours to suck away my soul. Where would I be if I worked there a year or more?

I would be a Barnyard.

I tried to guess who the Good Samaritan was who set loose Nard's turtle. Wade seemed sympathetic enough to do it.

Why didn't I do it? The question should have concerned me.

The full-time parking area outside the maintenance shop was empty but for one hideous Toyota pickup truck and a late model black Ford Explorer.

I walked into the shop and saw Barnyard standing oddly on his tip toes in the center of the floor facing me. Everyone else had gone home. As I got closer, he drifted in a circle. I then saw the chain hoist hook in his back belt loop. Somebody clipped him to the hoist and raised him just high enough so his dirty white sock toes scraped the floor. They threw the chain up over the I-beam so he had no way to lower himself.

"What the hell, Barnyard?"

"Lower me down." *Snock.*

I looked down at his grimy white socks. "Where are your shoes?"

He pointed out the door to a steel rack. Somebody had tied them together, thrown them across the rack and set them on fire. Now they were just dangling strips of melted, smoldering rubber and duct tape.

"Lower me down," he ordered me, "my pants are up in my ass and they're killin' me."

I looked up at the chain. It was hopelessly out of reach. "I don't know Barnyard. I can't reach the chain."

Tex suddenly stuck his head around the corner of the tool cage. The poor guy must live in that miserable prison cell. "Did you guys hear the news?" he shouted before he noticed Barnyard's predicament. "What the hell are you doing, Barnyard?"

"Let me down dammit. My ass is killing me."

"What news?" I asked.

"The memo just came out." Tex waved a sheet of paper. "The general manager just resigned. And the park is closing in thirty minutes. I don't know if it's for the rest of the day or forever. Who the hell hooked you on the chain hoist, Barnyard?"

Dink suddenly burst from the office door, startling me. He looked peculiarly at Barnyard. Then he looked at me. Tex ducked back behind the cage to avoid detection.

"The man is dead."

"Which one?" I asked, looking at his plastic clip-on tie.

"The actor that fell out of the Scrambler. They told me he was in a commercial for Pepsi a few years ago. Blunt trauma."

"That's a damn shame."

Dink pointed at me, like he did Josh earlier. "You need to talk to Morey about Byram killing himself."

"Already did. I just came from there."

Dink lowered his finger and looked wistful for a moment. "I had Hutton figured for beating himself to death with a baseball bat, or a vitamin overdose, not driving into a lake."

Well, Byram was full of surprises.

"Peterson the park general manager just quit." Dink was full of news I already knew. "County deputies are on their way here to make an arrest."

Now that I did not know. "For what?"

"Either embezzling or having an affair with a fifteen-year-old games attendant. Who the hell knows."

I wondered if Peterson was going to stop at a gas station on his way to his 25,000-square-foot home on the country club golf course and sit with a gun in his mouth, daring himself to pull the trigger, like Bob the guy with the snake on his face.

"Everything's gone crazy," Dink realistically concluded of the day's festivities. He looked at me. "Where are the rest of the guys?"

I looked at the time clock. It thunked 6:30 p.m. "I imagine they're all at home with their families now."

Dink leaned against a tool cabinet and rubbed his eyes. "They're all in for an ugly surprise when they come to work tomorrow."

"Why?"

Barnyard slowly drifted in a circle to look at Dink, the seat of his pants drawn relentlessly into his stupid bumblebee ass. Dink didn't seem to notice he was helplessly hanging on a belt loop from a chain hoist in his sock feet.

"Well I hate to tell you guys, but the park is shutting down indefinitely and laying everyone off, effective in about thirty minutes."

I expected a holy moly there Andy from Barnyard but it didn't happen. He was in shock, both from the news and his wedgie.

"Shutting down for good?" I asked.

"Yep," Dink answered. "Everything's closing and they are playing an announcement now for all the guests to head for the front gate. We're in deep shit. We're being investigated by just about every state and county enforcement agency and oversight commission there is. The head of the county building permit department told a local radio station an hour ago that we're killing, injuring and sickening more people than we are entertaining. Over three hundred guests show symptoms of food poisoning. Some reporter poking around the park landfill found about a hundred car batteries stacked on the ground, leaking acid, that were supposed to have been hauled away years ago. There are a thousand dead fish floating on Ford Lake. The county sheriff is padlocking the main gates at midnight after all the seasonal employees leave."

Leaking batteries on the ground? Now I knew where the coffee came from.

"We're getting severance pay, right?" Barnyard demanded from his hook.

"Don't count on it Barnyard," Dink blurted, angrily pointing at him. "You took all those bolts out of the Gator track, causing that accident. I should kick your ass while you're hangin ..."

Suddenly outside there was a blinding flash followed by an enormous gut-churning detonation that rattled the entire building. The lights blinked a couple times. We all ducked as dirt and dust showered us from the ceiling and the swaying fluorescent fixtures. Barnyard couldn't duck, he could only drift in a circle on his toes.

My guess was that some guy carrying the bomb Lloyd maybe thought he saw this morning actually got in and set it off. Or, more realistically, the broken gas line just destroyed the employee cafeteria.

Dink raised his head. He looked puzzled at me then hustled out of the shop around a corner toward the paint department in the opposite end of the building. The time clock clunked and reset itself after the power interruption.

Dirt and chunks of cafeteria debris suddenly started showering the parking area outside the big door like a calving glacier, banging and thumping on the vehicles. Canned and boxed goods rained like deafening hailstones on the shop roof and on the ground. A mangled refrigerator door crashed to the ground just outside the shop. Then a huge industrial gas stove fell out of the sky and slammed down on the black Ford Explorer, utterly demolishing the cab. The Explorer's emergency lights flashed flaccidly a few times then stopped.

Three minutes later Dink came back in carrying three brand new buckets of paint. He came over toward us, set them down, then walked over and kicked Barnyard in the ass, really hard. Then a second time.

Barnyard yelped in pain and tried to drift in a circle to avoid him. There was nothing else he could do. Dink merely gently turned him back around and kicked him a third time. A swirl of dust from the blast passed the big door.

"Get what you can while you can," Dink suggested as he carried the free paint out to what was once his black Ford Explorer.

"Let me down dammit. My ass is killin' me."

Outside I saw Dink stop, then slump to his knees when he looked in stunned shock at his ruined Explorer. That stolen paint saved his life.

"What the hell was that explosion!" Tex yelled from inside his cage. He was completely coated with grey dust. He looked like a golem.

"Gas leak," I responded lifelessly. I looked at Barnyard. "I wish I could help you. But I'm afraid I just ... don't care."

Snock. Barnyard spun to face the tool cage. "Tex come here and let me down my ass is killin' me."

I don't know if Tex let him down or not because I left. Just like that.

I walked to the time clock and realized I never got a time card from wacky, Hutton-worshipping Judy. I then smelled smoke and kerosene. I opened the adjacent hallway door and saw her file cabinets were all open and on fire. She must have done it on her way out.

Indifferent to this potential disaster, I closed the door, turned and walked through the back of the building through the electric shop, and then out the back door to the guard gate, bypassing what was once the employee cafeteria. I didn't feel like stealing anything or saying goodbye to anyone.

Unlike Judy's office, there was no fire at the cafeteria, and no one was inside at the time. The building was a pile of rubble. Only Morey stood beside it, staring, her shoulders slumped in pitiful resignation.

A brand-new silver Mercedes 300-series sedan blew past me to the gate. It was Peterson, the general manager, and he was a woman. And she was getting the hell out before the deputies arrived. She looked no more than twenty-five years old.

As she passed, I saw a young, pimply-faced boy in a games uniform in her passenger seat, and her back seat was loaded with lamps, a photocopier, boxes of office supplies and a plastic-wrapped platter of a hundred sub sandwich slices.

Free stuff.

This was a bad day.

Chapter 20: in which I leave for good but sort of find redemption

MY DAY ENDED right where it started – at guard gate 3. Gin blossom Lloyd and farm dog Walt had just come on duty for their overnight shift as I walked through. With the sun going down it was getting colder.

"Hi guys."

"You leaving or coming in?" Lloyd asked, not recognizing me. "We have a memo that says nobody is supposed to be let in. The park's closed for good."

I stopped to chat. "I'm going out, don't worry. That's why I'm walking *out* to my car."

"Did you hear that explosion?" Lloyd asked me.

"Yes, a guy with a bomb snuck in this morning and set it off."

Lloyd was nonplussed. "No, no. If somebody tried to walk in here with a bomb, I would have caught them. We were trained for that after that retired fella a few years back came in naked with a gun and shot himself."

Bob the guy with the snake on his face forced a policy and training change. Good for him.

"I'm kidding, it was a gas leak." Lloyd didn't get it. "Nobody hurt, but the employee cafeteria is a pile of splinters right now."

The phone rang.

"And nobody was hurt?" Lloyd reacted. "That's a miracle."

"Well, I think Morey's feelings are hurt."

The phone rang again.

Nobody said hotline. Nobody was in the mood. Walt answered.

"Guard shack ... no, far as I know the park will be permanently closed. Yes, your husband has lost his job. We all have. Yea. Damn shame is what it is."

"With the cafeteria blowed up, I reckon we're going to have to eat somewhere else then, Walt," Lloyd suggested as Walt hung up. "But one less building they'll have to winterize when they shut down."

Walt nodded and stepped back out. "I don't know how some of the workers are going to tell their families the park closed and they've been fired. That's a terrible thing to have to tell your family."

"Maybe they could hire you to do it, Walt," I sarcastically suggested. "Like you just did to that family."

"Well hell, Walt, you and I are next," Lloyd speculated. "They aren't going to keep old guys like us around. They'll be coming out any minute to kick us to the curb. They'll hire a young guy from an agency to patrol the perimeter a couple times a night until the park reopens, if it ever does. Lucky for me ..." Lloyd paused as a pair of headlights turned down at the far end of the parking lot and slowly approached.

"... I can get Medicare."

Let there be light.

We all three stepped aside to let the thirty-year-old grease truck creep past the guard shack, possibly for the last time. It was still in hideous shape. Three guys were still stuffed in the cab, bundled in corduroy coats, caps and rain gear. They still looked through the filthy window at me as they crept by.

They were going to park the truck and go home for good, just like me and everybody else.

"Damn that grease truck stinks," Lloyd commented. "Where you reckon those guys will get jobs driving grease trucks?"

"Hey Lloyd, you celebrate your work anniversary with Helen this morning when you got off?" Walt asked.

"I didn't celebrate nothing," Lloyd responded flatly. "I was shootin' pool with a rope. Helen told me to just take her home."

The phone rang again. Walt answered "guard shack" then lowered his voice.

I think I know how Barnyard got strung up. Before Lump went home, he made good on his promise. He grabbed Barnyard when he wasn't expecting it and hooked his pants to the chain hoist, pulling him up high enough so his feet just brushed the floor.

It was black and blue titty payback.

While he was hanging there helpless, that evil Craft-Tech tool guy also made good on his promise and removed Barnyard's rotten shoes. He tied the strings together, threw them over the steel rack, doused them in lighter fluid and set them on fire. Just like he said he would do. Although there was no evidence he beat Barnyard with them first.

"Were we supposed to let those guys in?" Lloyd asked no one of the grease truck crew. "We aren't supposed to let anybody in. The park is closed."

Walt hung up the phone and stepped out of the shack. "That was Morey. Somebody set all the filing cabinets in the maintenance administrator's office on fire. They got it put out but all the maintenance records are destroyed. Not sure who did it. Damn shame."

I knew. Of course, I knew. I was the smartest motherfucker this park ever hired.

"I'm glad that SOB Hutton is dead," I pronounced in a firm voice, taking Morey's advice. "There I said it. Like they say in Texas, he needed killing. He was insane."

I felt no better about what I just did. No happiness, no sorrow. I was as dead inside as Byram was on the slab down at the funeral home. Maybe I needed Merv's prayer and Bible study more than I thought. Too bad it was now ancient history.

The guards looked curiously at me.

"Mr. Hutton is dead?" Lloyd asked.

I arrived this morning ready to be the most conscientious rides maintenance guy in the world. I had visions of becoming a state-certified amusement device inspector. I had prospects.

I turned toward my car. "Take care, guys."

I heard Lloyd ask Walt, "what happened to Mr. Hutton?"

I never saw Walter, the boss who hired me. I never got to prove to him I knew the difference between a hammer and a screwdriver. I guess he went home before the park closed for good. He'll come back in the morning and find the gates padlocked. His abrupt unemployment will surely make him forget about me.

I know in advance about the padlocked gates. It will save me the trip. Remember, I was the smartest guy in the park.

Take that, Byram – you and your drowned, dead ass.

I walked toward my car in the seasonal employee parking lot, right where I left it somewhere between fourteen hours and twenty years ago. The last yogurt raisin in the box. The left rear tire looked low.

"Would you look at that!" I heard farm dog Walt suddenly bark. I turned to look. Nard's turtle was passing through the guard gate, its head held high. "Where did that turtle come from?"

Nard's turtle and I both managed to escape Burkewood Fun Park with our lives. Even though he was so old he had moss on his shell he didn't stop until he was outside that gate. No one at the park was going to take his life or his dignity. I was impressed.

"He'd be good eatin'," Lloyd observed.

Then, that made me realize that I was still letting the park take not my life but a crucial part – my compassion. During my rambunctious college days, I screamed about empathy and tolerance toward others. It would be hypocritical to let that part of me die now, after only one day. I resolved to not let Burkewood have that power, and that control gave me a weird feeling of new-found confidence and positivity.

Tomorrow, I would start the job search all over and pretend this day never happened.

But there was still an unresolved issue. I looked back one last time at the two guards. They were spellbound by Nard's turtle walking with purpose out the gate.

"Hey," I shouted. They looked at me. "Do either of you know the secret of stepping off a moving Carousel without killing yourself?"

"Sure," Lloyd responded, arching backward. "You just lean way back, like this, when you step off."

Huh.

I got in my car and left.

GET TO KNOW ME

Dale M. Brumfield is an anti-death penalty advocate, award-winning journalist, erstwhile adjunct professor, "American Grotesk" historyteller and cultural archaeologist. Dale received his MFA in fiction from Virginia Commonwealth University in 2015, and writes for numerous publications nationwide. He also worked almost twenty years in the theme park industry, where he learned and closely guarded the secret of safely stepping off a moving Carousel.

Thanks to all my Richmond, Virginia supporters and Theme Park Babylon blog readers. Special thanks to the incredible Susan, and the greatest kids in the world, Hunter, Jackson and Hollis. What a ride.

#Americangrotesk

#10years10books

www.ingramcontent.com/pod-product-compliance
Lightning Source LLC
Chambersburg PA
CBHW021400290426
44108CB00010B/325